THE WORLD
NEEDS
MEDJUGORJE
NOW MORE THAN EVER

THE WORLD
NEEDS
MEDJUGORJE
NOW MORE THAN EVER

RITA SILVESTRI

CITI OF
BOOKS

Dear Readers,

Moving Forward

When I wrote this book two years ago I did not realize how much the landscape of our world would change in such a short time. Many lives are in an upheaval. Our values are no longer valued. However, before I begin to detail what I want to say, please remember, believers, that God already has prevailed and as Christ, Our Savior, said to Peter when he established His church here on earth, "The Gates of Hell shall not prevail against it".

So many of us are living lives that we hardly recognize because the world we were born into no longer exists. Abortion is rampant; sixty one million babies + have been destroyed in and out of their mother's wombs since Roe vs. Wade was passed in the seventies. Today the Supreme Court of our land has said that marriage between a man and a woman is unconstitutional. Christmas is no longer celebrates the birth of Christ. It is now an economic holiday. Christians throughout the world are beheaded for their faith. Divorces are in, traditional marriage is out. Who knows what that will bring. TV touts porn. Laws allowing euthanasia and assisted suicide are cropping up all over the country. Businesses collapse, there are killings and riots in the streets; our right to bear arms may soon be a thing of the past along with the Constitution of our country. Men and women in the military are maligned; families now consist of one parent or two parents of the same sex. Churches are empty and military chaplains are punished or chastised for saying the name of Jesus.

Lust has replaced love and morality. Decency, chastity and modesty are considered worthless values. How did we get here? We lost God somewhere along the way. He has not abandoned us, we have abandoned Him. For this reason I decided to republish my book, The World Needs Medjugorje and rename it The World Needs Medjugorje, Now More than Ever. I hope that it will reach a new audience or be read again by those who saw it's worth the first time. Dear Readers, please read and enjoy learning about the fruits and messages of Medjugorje. Ask God not to let evil prevail against our world and His church. Ask Him bring to peace to all of us and our loved ones here in our world today.

Thank you. May God Bless You.

Rita Silvestri

DEDICATION

This book is dedicated to my beloved patron saint, Sister Rita of Cassia, who protected me and walked beside me during my entire life even when I had no idea that she was there. Saint Rita introduced me to God, my Father, my Savior Jesus Christ,
The Holy Spirit, my constant companion, and my dearest Mother Mary.

"Especially little children, pray for the gifts of the Holy Spirit so that in the spirit of love, every day and in each situation, you may be closer to your fellow-man; and that in wisdom and love you may overcome every difficulty."
Thank you for responding to my call.

Message : May 25, 2000

CITIOFBOOKS, INC.
3736 Eubank NE Suite A1
Albuquerque, NM 87111-3579
www.citiofbooks.com
Hotline: 1 (877) 389-2759
Fax: 1 (505) 930-7244

Ordering Information:
Quantity sales. Special discounts are available on quantity purchases by corporations, associations, and others. For details, contact the publisher at the address above.

Printed in the United States of America.

| ISBN-13: | Softcover | 979-8-89391-495-5 |
| | eBook | 979-8-89391-496-2 |

Library of Congress Control Number: 2024927093

TABLE OF CONTENTS

MEDJUGORJE

A BEAUTIFUL LITTLE VILLAGE set high in the rock covered mountains of Croatia in an area of the world that once was a part of the former Yugoslavia, ruled under the iron fist of Marshall Tito, a Socialist Dictator from 1943 until 1991. Medjugorje is in Croatia, which is situated in Southeastern Europe across the Adriatic Sea from Italy. Contained within the boundaries of Croatia, is the Federation of Bosnia-Herzegovina, where in the late nineteen hundreds was fought a brutal and bloody civil war. The people living in this rugged land above the sparkling sea are for the most part either Christian or Muslim. Both are fierce in their religious beliefs and ethnic culture.

Follow the author, Rita Silvestri, as she heeds the call of the Holy Mother of God and journeys to the Village of Medjugorje to witness the apparitions, which began in 1981. She lives the miracles and the challenges of Medjugorje today. Meet the pilgrims with whom she has traveled. Listen to the visionaries and hear firsthand the words of Our Lady. Walk with Rita among the people of this land, where the Queen of Peace reigns, and where love presides in the hearts of those who come in response to her invitation. Become one with those of all faiths, who travel from far off places to hear the messages that Mary brings from her Son to the place where heaven and earth are joined as one.

INTRODUCTION

IN MID-JUNE OF 1981, a major life changing event was about to take place in the lives of every person living in a little parish in the mountains above the Adriatic Sea. This event would come to impact the entire world as we know it. And, today it still continues to play out. For how long, none of us knows. Mirjana and Ivanka, two teen aged girls were strolling together in an area almost totally unknown to the outside world at that time, the name of which can hardly be pronounced correctly even by those who have traveled there.

The place is called Medjugorje. Those of us, who have traveled on pilgrimages together, say Med-ju-gor-ee-uh. Hopefully, this will make it easier for you to pronounce it as your read about the events that have transpired in this holy place over the past thirty plus years. Because of what occurred on that peaceful day in 1981, thousands of pilgrims flock to the site, while many others still wonder where it is and how to get there.

When traveling to Medjugorje, one has to fly to the beautiful country of Croatia in Southeastern Europe and into either the cities of Split or Dubrovnik, both of which are located on the coastline of the Adriatic Sea. Another choice would be to fly to Sarajevo, which is located inland within the confines of the Federation of BosniaHercegovina along with Mostar and Medjugorje. Many of us heard of Bosnia-Hercegovina in the 90's because of the civil war which ravaged the area at that time. Part of the country as we know it today was called Yugoslavia. The conflict devastated the land, its people and its way of life. The village of Medjugorje was saved from destruction because of the intervention of Our Holy Mother who covered it with clouds to prevent military pilots from sighting their targets.

Croatia, as well as The Federation of Bosnia-Hercegovina, now occupies the land which was once Yugoslavia. Approximately eighty nine percent of the people living in that part of the world are Croatian. The remainder of the population, to the best of my knowledge, consists of Serbs, Slovenians and Macedonians, along with other small ethnic groups.

Now that you know what to call this beautiful place, I hope it will be easier for you to read about the memories and miracles I have to share with you. Come with me, the two young women and the others who were to join them as this story takes you through the coming days, weeks and years since it all began. On the day of June 24, 1981, the Holy Mother of God would begin thirty plus years of apparitions in Medjugorje to six young people who are now adults with families. The youngest visionary, as they are now known, has entered his forties and the oldest are approaching their fifties. They are people like us, living lives such as our own and dealing not only with the difficulties in this Godless world, but with Our Mother's visits, which eventually brought millions of pilgrims to their quiet little world.

PROLOGUE

ON A WARM SUMMER day in Eastern Europe, two teenage girls, much like all other young girls throughout the world were walking together and discussing what most girls just like them discuss, boys. They were friends and their names were Mirjana (Mir-yana) and Ivanka (E-von-ka). From what I have heard, they also had in mind to smoke a cigarette or two away from the prying eyes of family. So, they strolled together to the base of Mount Podbrdo (Pod-bor-do), a high, rocky hill located in a tiny village called Bijakovici (Bee-ya-ko-ve-chee). Thirty plus years ago, what was about to happen in this quiet place was destined to change the world forever.

As the girls chatted at the base of the hill, Ivanka glanced up and saw what looked like the figure of a beautiful young woman standing above them, a short distance away from where she and Mirjana stood. Not exactly sure of what she was seeing, but thinking it was the Virgin Mary, she told her friend that Gospa, the Creation word for the Mother of God, was up on Podbrdo. Mirjana scoffed at the suggestion thinking that Ivanka was trying to be funny. She told Ivanka that she was wrong and asked why in the world the Mother of God would ever appear to the likes of them. It would be impossible. Without even looking up, she then urged Ivanka to walk on, which they both did. As they moved away, they were hailed by another teen, their friend, Milka, the sister of a girl named Marija (Maria). Milka was looking for someone to help herd her grandmother's goats.

After Milka joined them, the girls returned to the place where they had been standing when Ivanka thought she saw the Holy Mother. At that moment, all three saw the beautiful Lady. This was the only time Milka would ever share this experience with the others. By now, a fourth girl named Vicka (Vish-Ka) had arrived and joined the group. Vicka lived just a short distance from the hill near the home of Ivanka. Mirjana was not from Medjugorje. She had come from Sarajevo to spend the summer months with her grandmother. Milka and her sister, Marija, lived in the area with their grandmother.

When Vicka saw the Lady on the hill, she became very frightened and ran home. On her way, she met up with two more friends, boys, each of whom was named Ivan (E-von). When Vicka told them what she had seen, they begged her to go back with them to where she had said the Mother of God stood. When they saw the figure who beckoned them to come to her, Ivan Dragicevic (who was later to become a visionary) left the scene and took off running toward his home, just as Vicka had. That evening the bewildered and frightened young people all shared what they had witnessed with their parents and grandparents; much to the concern of all. The news quickly spread throughout the village. Parents, grandparents, relatives, neighbors and young friends all had much difficulty believing the story. Milka's grandmother would never allow her to return to the hill again. She is not counted among the visionaries. I have been told that she suffered greatly because of this.

The next day four of the children went back to the hill. They were curious and hoping to see the beautiful young woman again. When the other children returned to the place, where they had seen the vision, Vicka brought along little Jacov Colo, who was barely ten at the time. She also brought another friend, Marija, Milka's sister. These two children also saw the Lady. Ivan Dragicevic, who had run away initially, returned to the scene. Ivan Ivankovic did not. And so the six visionaries, Mirjana, Ivanka, Marija, Vicka, Ivan and Jacov were to begin a life graced with apparitions from Our Holy Mother.

The children approached the Gospa, as they knew her, on the hill. They asked why she was appearing to them since they were just ordinary people and not particularly good. She told them that was why she was coming to them. She chooses those who are not perfect and who need to be saved but in this little village she also found faith and devotion. She was coming to deliver messages of peace and salvation from Her Son to the world in this remote place through these young people who came to be called visionaries.

In the beginning, Our Lady told the visionaries that there were ten secrets she would deliver to each of them for the benefit of the world. These secrets would address things that would happen here on earth in the coming years. One secret has already been disclosed to the world. It addressed a permanent sign that would appear in the heavens announcing the coming of her Son. We are told that some of the secrets could be mitigated by prayer and it is my understanding that one already has. However, only the visionaries have the knowledge of that secret and the others they have been given.

The messages of conversion and peace are intended to bring the world back to God. The lives of the visionaries and the villagers evolved into what Medjugorje has become today. When those of us who have come to know Medjugorje think of our times there, we remember wonderful places and people. In our hearts we see Mt. Krizevac with its magnificent cross, built by the villagers in the 1930s. We think of Apparition Hill, the miracles of the sun, St. James Church and the multitudes of confessionals lining the large open patio next to it. We envision the outside altar behind St. James Church and remember seeing over five thousand people in attendance at the International Mass each evening. Our minds take us to the beautiful painting of our Holy Mother adorning the stage in the yellow building. There is the bronze statue of the Risen Christ and mysteries of the rosary on the path leading to the above ground graveyard in which Father Barbaric was laid to rest. There are the Blue Crosses, Cenacolo and the Castle. We remember Father Jozo Zovko, Father Svetozar Kraljevic, Father Slavko Barbaric, Patrick and Nancy Lotta, David Parkes and so many others. You will meet them in the coming pages.

We pilgrims envision the main altar inside the church often filled with at least thirty five or more priests during each mass. In my mind, I can see them coming down off the altar and spreading out into the throngs of pilgrims from all over the world to bring the Body and Blood of Our Beloved Savior to the hundreds, even thousands of faithful waiting patiently inside and outside of the church. We all think of the visionaries and remember the words of Our Mother's messages delivered to us from them each day. We miss all of the devout people with whom we have found deep friendships and we see the beauty in the groups who pray together as they walk through the vineyards on the way to daily mass. We watch as the sun sets, dances and pulsates before us and the sky fills with heavenly colors not of this earth. Most of all, we feel the closeness of our God and our Mother in this extraordinary place only a breath away from heaven.

1

IN THE BEGINNING

THE APPARITIONS WILL CONTINUE until God chooses to bring the Messages of Medjugorje to an end here on earth. Believers from all over the world see what is happening in Medjugorje as the beginning of the End Times as foretold in the Bible when, as the chosen children of God, we will stand together. We will be like the visionaries who were not all friends when the events of June 24, 1981 took place. Some knew each other, the others did not. Some came from different places and they all had separate personalities and diverse lives.

Vicka Ivankovic-Mijatovic was born on September 3, 1964 in Bijakovici in a stone house a very short distance from the home of Ivanka. Our Holy Mother has directed Vicka to pray for the sick. Vicka, herself, has been sick most of her life and has suffered greatly. During a trip to Medjugorje in October of 2010, I had the privilege of visiting the home of her youth and seeing the room in which our Holy Mother visited Vicka during a difficult and painful time in her life. Vicka was in the hospital the very day I spent time in her childhood home. Later that evening I spoke with her sister who informed me that Vicka had returned from the hospital that afternoon and was doing better. Vicka understands pain and offers it up for those whose lives are as difficult. In spite of her suffering, she is always smiling. Vicka comes from a family of seven brothers and sisters. These days she lives in a small town outside of Medjugorje with her husband Mario and their two children, a son and a daughter. She continues to have daily visits from Our Holy Mother and has been given nine secrets.

Marija Pavlovic-Lunetti was born on April 1, 1965. Her prayers are said for the souls in purgatory. On the 25th of each month, Our Mother gives Marija a public message for the world. Marija continues to see Mary every day. She has been given nine secrets. At the time of the apparitions she was attending school in Mostar while she and her sister Milka were living with her Grandmother. Marija is married and has four children. She and her husband and their family live in Italy.

Jacov Colo, at the age of ten, the youngest of the six was born on March 6, 1971 in Sarajevo. He lost his mother in September of 1983 and saw little of his father, who left the family and worked in Germany. At the time of his mother's death he went to live with his uncle. Jacov, who has been given all ten secrets, sees Our Mother Mary on Christmas Day each year. He is also allowed to see the Infant Jesus. He, along with Vicka, prays for the sick. Jacov and Vicka were taken together to see both heaven and hell. Of the six visionaries, Jacov is the only one who has never said whether he will be alive when the permanent sign appears in Medjugorje. He says only that it is a secret.

Jacov lives just across the street from Mirjana. On my first trip to Medjugorje, I passed his house daily where he lives with his wife Annalisa and their three children. Their home is just down the road from Ivan's place where I was staying. Jacov had two beautiful little dogs, who would run out and bark. My friends and I loved to stop and play with them, hoping to someday meet Jacov who always appears shy.

Mirjana once told me that I was not correct when I said that about Jacov. Apparently, he has quite a sense of humor. One day a group of us listened to Jacov speak from his front yard. In his face I could see the child that he had been at the time of the start of the apparitions. How Our Mother must love him, what mother could resist?

Ivanka Ivankovich-Elez, the youngest of the girls, was born on July 21, 1966. Ivanka prays for families. Her mother died in 1981 shortly before the apparitions began. Ivanka asked the Gospa if her mother was taken to heaven to be with God. The answer was yes. Our Lady allowed Ivanka not only the knowledge that her mother was with God, but I have read that she also reunited mother and daughter as many as five times over the years. Ivanka has an apparition every year on June 25th the anniversary of the apparitions. This is the day that all six of the children first saw Our Mother together. Ivanka is married, has three children and lives in Medjugorje with her family.

Mirjana Dragicevic-Soldo, was born in Sarajevo on March 18, 1965. She was studying at the university during the summer of 1981. When the apparitions began, Mirjana was spending the summer with her grandmother in Bijakovici. Mirjana told my husband and I, when we were blessed to meet her at a conference in Las Vegas several years ago, that before her friend Ivanka saw Our Holy Mother on Apparition Hill, she, Mirjana, had never known anything about any apparitions anywhere including Lourdes and Fatima. Later, I heard that none of the other children had either.

Mirjana lives across the street from Jacov. Jacov lives next door to the house in which we stay each time we make the pilgrimage to Medjugorje. One can stay with Mirjana as I stayed in the house of Ivan on my first visit. It is quite an honor to be in such a heavenly neighborhood. Mirjana is married to Marko Soldo and they have two daughters. She has been asked by our Holy Mother to pray for the unbelievers whom Mirjana describes as those who do not know God's love. She has been given all ten secrets and sees our Holy Mother on the second of each month.

Ivan, the older of the two boys, was born on May 25, 1965. He prays for the youth of the world and for priests. Our Lady has revealed nine secrets to Ivan and appears to him daily. She once asked Ivan if he would like to learn what his future held in store. He said he would.

Ivan has said that he is not sorry to know and has indicated that he is confident and not afraid of what he was told. He thinks that all people should feel that way. Ivan lives one half of the year in Medjugorje and the remainder in Boston. He and his wife, Laureen, who is an American, have four children.

Sometimes referred to as the seventh visionary as time went on, Father Jozo (Joseph) Zovko, Pastor of the Church of St. James in Medjugorje, was away when the apparitions began. He did not believe the children's stories upon his return to his parish. At that time, the Bishop of Mostar did believe their testimonies. The Bishop was sensitive to their situation and was doing as much as he could to support and comfort the children and their families. Time would change his thoughts and actions.

Father Jozo, on the other hand, questioned them together and separately trying to discern the truth. When word spread of the happenings on the hill, the authorities, who were communists, took the children away one by one for interrogation. Very soon, thereafter, they began to live a life of harsh treatment. They were all mercilessly questioned, sometimes together, sometimes separately, but their accounts never varied. No amount of force, no threats of death or bodily harm, either to themselves or their families, could persuade them to change their stories. Even ten year old Jacov never wavered in his description of what he had seen or heard. Not one of the children would deny the appearance of Our Holy Mother, even under fear of severe punishment. Each was secure in the fact that Mary was who she said she was and that she would protect them. Their stories all coincided. It was what it was.

The young visionaries were relentlessly pursued by the police and subjected to all sorts of physical and mental tests and examinations; some of which could have been construed as torture. They often had to hide in order escape police scrutiny. There were stretches on the road, which runs along the base of Apparition Hill, where they would be aware that the police were following them and that they had no place to hide. The Blessed Mother would tell them to stay there in spite of the fact that they were out in the open. Our Lady would cover them with her mantle to make them invisible to those searching for them. This often happened at 5:40 in the afternoon, the time when she appeared to them daily. Today this area is dotted by blue crosses to mark all the spots where they, stood shielded by her in those frightening moments.

In time the Bishop of the Mostar Diocese, where Medjugorje was located, began to turn against the visionaries. He refused to believe that what they attested to was true. At about the same time, Father Jozo started to believe them. The Holy Mother had come to Father Joso and instructed him to protect the children. There is a movie about Medjugorje, which was made after these events took place, and stars Martin Sheen. It is called The Miracle of Medjugorje.

A scene in the film depicts a story that many of us who know Medjugorje have heard. It describes the afternoon when Father Jozo was in the church and heard the children running toward the doors calling for help. He looked out and was confronted by their cries that the police were chasing them and were not far behind. Father Jozo quickly gathered the visionaries inside and instructed them to hide. Seconds later the police were pounding on the door. When he responded to their knocks, they asked Father if he had seen the children and he answered truthfully that he had. They never asked another question and simply decided that the youngsters had encountered the priest and continued to flee through the fields. The police ran on in pursuit of the visionaries who were safely hidden away inside the church.

Because he protected the visionaries and his church a decision, which amounted to crimes against the regime, the police arrested Father Jozo. They kept him imprisoned for eighteen months. They tortured, beat him, and kept him in alone in darkness for much of the time. They also took away his priestly rights to celebrate Mass and consecrate the Eucharist.

The original amount of time set for his imprisonment, as an enemy of the state, was to have been much longer, but when the officials in charge of his confinement discovered that many of the guards assigned to him were converting to Catholicism, they shortened his sentence. He was released after only eighteen months, however, eighteen very long months due to the conditions of his captivity. Upon his release, he was sent away to a small church in the beautiful town of Tihaljina (Tee-ha-lena) in Bosnia-Hercegovina. This church is located in rolling hills about 30 kilometers outside of Medjugorje. Fr. Joso was there for a relatively short time. But while he was there, something very interesting happened.

I was told an interesting tale, which I will share with you. I hope it is true, but if it is not, it is still lovely to think about. As the story goes, the parish priest (Father Jozo?) had seen an extremely beautiful statue of the Virgin Mary in Rome and wanted to buy it for his church. However, there was a financial problem. The parishioners did not have the money to purchase the statue. They had been saving their collections to repair the roof of the church. Interestingly, the roof and the statue would cost exactly the same amount of money. After much discussion, the decision to buy the statue took precedence over the repair of the roof. The statue was ordered and shipped from Rome. Once the statue was delivered and installed in the church, the roof was no longer in need of repair. Miraculous? I have no idea. I never heard that part of the story. However, as I have heard it said (on Fox News), "I report, you decide".

Father Jozo did not remain in Tihaljina for very long before he was sent off again to another parish, this time to the church in Siroki (Siro-ke) Brijeg (Bre-jig). There is a seminary in this beautiful mountain area which was a scene of martyrdom in the 1940's. When visiting Medjugorje, it is essential that this location be numbered among your destinations of prayer and visitation. Siroki Brijeg is about 20 kilometers outside of Medjugorje.

It is also the scene of much goodness on the part of Father Jozo as he set about to rebuild the lives of the people who lost everything during the civil war, which tore through the region in the early part of the

1990's. Although, Father Jozo was not allowed to return to St. James Parish, he continued to shepherd and support the people of Croatia, particularly after the bloody war that tore the country apart in the early 1990's and beyond.

"Dear Children,

Also today I call you to prayer, especially today when satan wants war and hatred. I call you anew, little children; pray and fast that God may give you peace, witness peace to every heart and be carriers of peace in this world without peace.

I am with you and intercede before God for each of you. Do not be afraid because the one who prays is not afraid of evil and has no hatred in the heart. Thank you for having responded to my call."

Message: September 25, 2001

2

BEYOND THE BEGINNING

A S A PILGRIM ON my first trip to Medjugorje, I was able to visit the beautiful church of Our Lady of the Assumption located high in the hills in the idyllic setting of the small town of Siroki Brijeg to which Father Jozo was sent after Tihaljina. It is a quiet peaceful mountain area today, but it is also where thirty Franciscan priests and Seminarians were martyred by barbaric and sadistic soldiers who stormed the seminary at the end of the Second World War. It is a very sobering experience to visit the scene of this horrible bloody massacre where the priests and young seminarians were subjected to unspeakable terror before being murdered. They were herded together, told to remove their habits and crucifixes and stomp on them, which they refused to do. They were brutally tortured then led at gun point to an underground man made cave and shot, after which they were doused with petrol and torched, while in some cases still alive. Even describing this to you having seen the photos taken after the atrocities and the horrors that occurred there makes my soul cry.

Inside the church there are also photographs of all those who suffered and died. One can see these photos as well as read the biographies of each. Some of them were still very young; many I believe still in their late teens. There were others in their prime and those who had served their God almost to the end of their natural lives here on earth. It is a hard picture to erase from your mind once you realize what these saintly men endured.

If you so choose, you can go down into the cave and see firsthand that to which these men of God were subjected. For me the cave still carried the stench and sounds of brutality. I feel that we need to see and experience these things to understand the suffering and hideous cruelty that mankind can impose when under the power of satan. He does exist and we need to understand him to grasp the meaning of hell. Please note that the name of satan is not capitalized. I refuse to afford him any special recognition.

As I mentioned in the previous chapter, Father Jozo continued to work with his community in Siroki Brijeg and established a refuge for families torn apart by the civil war that demolished the region. He gave a whole new meaning to Siroki Brijeg by replacing the evil of the attack with holiness. He took in displaced women and their children, the widows and orphans who had lost husbands, fathers, sons and brothers in the war. Because of the tremendous needs of those affected by the conflict, Father Jozo started the Godparent Program to raise funds in order to provide food, clothing, shelter, education and protection for the survivors. He established schools for the children, provided housing for the homeless and work for the destitute. Many of the people on our pilgrimages fostered those in need and went back year after year to visit the families who had become one with theirs. Our tour leader in the early days, Nevis Jelich, was responsible for putting together the American representatives of the Godparent program. Margaret and Tom Eckroth from my the parish in St. George, Utah were among the first to become part of the group. Tom still leads a prayer group dedicated to Our Lady of Peace each Tuesday morning at nine in the church.

I mentioned earlier that the Bishop of Mostar turned his back on the Visionaries, as did his successor after his death. It is only an opinion of mine that his change of heart came purely out of fear of possible retaliation by the communistic government. I have nothing solid which could ever help me prove that point. It is simply what I feel in my heart after having read a great deal about the conditions which exist there. The

Bishop might have followed in the footsteps of Father Jozo and could have been imprisoned had he proclaimed the apparitions approved by the church. Rome has been studying the situation in Medjugorje for years according to what we have been told.

I feel that God has His reason for what is happening today. Catholics are allowed to go there as believers and so are our priests and bishops. The clergy cannot, however, lead pilgrimages. Neither Pope has visited Medjugorje. It is said that the Holy Father must be invited by the Bishop of the Diocese of Mostar. He, the Bishop, is the Head of the Church in Medjugorje so only he can issue the invitation. If you ask ten different people the same question about why Medjugorje has not been approved by the church and why the Holy Father has never been there, you will get ten different answers. I am not an authority on the situation and I certainly have none. Only God knows the real reasons for what transpires there and in His time we will be given the answers. Until then we are free to accept or deny the fruits of Medjugorje, of which there are many.

I find it interesting that Father Jozo, who initially denied that the visionaries were actually seeing apparitions, became one of them in the eyes of the faithful as time went on. I was once introduced to this priest and I felt that I had met a saint on earth. My husband travels with me to Medjugorje and we no longer see or hear much of Father Jozo. The Godparent Program no longer exists. On our last two trips we were told that there was no need for it to continue. The people are able to care for themselves. The orphaned children are grown, educated and off on their own. As for Father Jozo, it is my understanding that he left Siroki Brijeg and entered a monastery in Austria for some much needed rest. I have also heard that he is traveling with Cardinal Schoenborn, Archbishop of Vienna. Cardinal Schoenborn is thought to be considered as a possible candidate to be the next Pope upon the death of Pope Benedict XVI. If so, Father Jozo is in good company. There is much information to sift through one never knows what is fact or what is fiction.

Through all of the years since the beginning, life in Medjugorje has continued to change rapidly. The visionaries are now adults and Father Jozo is no longer there. Another priest to have a very profound influence at St. James Parish from the early times was Father Slavko Barbaric. He began working with the people of Medjugorje around January of 1982. Father Barbaric was a brilliant writer of many books which have been sold by the millions all over the world. He was highly educated, spoke many languages and was loved by all who knew him.

He died suddenly in the year 2000 after ascending Mt. Krizevac (Kreez-vak) or as we know it, Cross Mountain, praying the Way of the Cross. He collapsed near the top of the mountain, just below the cross shortly after the climb. There is a memorial dedicated to Father Barbaric in that location. Prayer requests are left there. Parishioners of St. James Church lovingly carried his body down to the village after his death.

Shortly before his demise, it appeared that he too might be imprisoned by the government as was Father Jozo. His death prevented that from happening. Many accounts indicate that this good priest knew he would die soon. Father Barbaric was only forty four years old when he left this life, but he had touched many lives with the truth of the Lord through his books and his love. When the visionaries asked the Holy Mother if Father Slavcko was in heaven, she assured them that he was with her and that she had come for him. Father Barbaric is buried a short distance behind St. James Church in an above ground marble coffin. My husband, Nate, and I visit his tomb each year when we are in Medjugorje.

Pilgrims from all over the world began to descend upon this remote place where people tended their animals, crops of tobacco and grapes.

The old way of life slowly ceased to exist. As time went on, the children grew closer to Our Holy Mother. They met with her in many places and were observed not only by the police, but by the curious, many of whom were not of the Catholic faith. There was literally no room at the inn for the hoards of visitors who had traveled great distances knowing they would have no place to stay upon arrival. Parents, grandparents, relatives, friends and neighbors of the children opened their homes to as many travelers as they could accommodate.

Through my work, in the US, I was acquainted with several people who had gone there in the early days as pilgrims. They shared with me that they were among those who slept three and four to a small bed; sometimes even sleeping on the floor. Rooms were added to houses as money was made available through donations. Italy is close to Croatia. Italians came to help with the building and renovations. In the beginning there was little in the way of hygienic facilities. Americans talked of having to use outhouses. I was amused when I heard this. My guess was that these people were going to this small isolated mountain area hoping to find at least a two star hotel. Americans in particular are an interesting people. Most of us cannot even imagine what it is like not to have even the most rudimentary of creature comforts. I even heard that some people complained because they could not find a place to brush their teeth or wash out clothing. Frankly, I have to admire them because they went anyway and by the thousands I might add. There is one thing of which I am certain now that I have met and lived among the people of Medjugorje; the early pilgrims must have eaten well in spite of the fact that places to stay were somewhat scarce. The villagers are kind, generous and caring people. I have to think that they did all that they could to put together delicious and plentiful meals for their guests. I cannot say that I have ever had more delicious food than that served by our host family with whom we stay.

When pilgrims saw what they journeyed to see, they stared in awe as they observed the children kneel in ecstasy before the Mother of God during their daily apparitions in church or wherever they were held without fear of reprisal. Those who come, still see the same things today in Medjugorje, if they open their hearts and souls to believe. But, some things are different. Our Holy Mother wanted some changes to come about in the habits and lives of the villagers. She told the farmers that they must stop growing tobacco and add more vines to their vineyards. At first the people were fearful of losing the income from their tobacco crops, but the grape vines quickly became lush and heavy with fruit, and before long the jugs of wine grew plentiful in Medjugorje. Tobacco is now a thing of the past in this blessed place. People still smoke, but I do not see tobacco growing anywhere and never have during the times I have visited. Strolling through the grape vines on the way to the church can be one of the most peaceful and delightful walks imaginable, especially if the harvest is in and a few of the sweetest grapes have been accidentally left behind. It is also very pleasant to watch the bountiful harvest being brought into the neighborhoods, which surround the area in which we stay. I had never seen the juice flowing from the grapes until I was privileged to watch a family stomping their harvest amid laughter and camaraderie. I was delighted to see that this particular family was using a big, round, plastic swimming pool.

I watch the people in Medjugorje and I also look for their dogs to photograph. Often, I love to stop for a moment to pet and talk with the dogs. I know they understand me and I feel their love in return. Medjugorje is so many things to me. I am happy there, but I am also happy at home because the blessings of Medjugorje follow me wherever I go. Medjugorje is just what I think heaven will be, bright and full of beauty, precious birds, plants, flowers and animals, who roam freely in addition to wonderful friends and joyful days filled to the brim with the love of God.

"Dear Children,

Also today I call you to pray, pray, pray. Only in prayer will you be near to me and my son, and you will see how short this life is. In your heart a desire for heaven will be born. Joy will begin to rule in your heart and prayer will begin to flow like a river. In your words there will be only thanksgiving to God for having created you and the desire for holiness will become a reality for you. Thank you for responding to my call."

Message: August 25, 2006

3

THE PERMANENT SIGN

WE KNOW THAT THE Mother of God has come to earth from Heaven to teach us peace and love. She has told us that we must convert and that through prayer, fasting, reconciliation, and the reading of scriptures some of the chastisement for the sins of mankind can be mitigated. Our Lady has said that we must eat of the Bread of Life, repent and confess our sins at least once a month. The more we pray, the more we confess and the closer we become to God, all of these things become easier and part of our daily spiritual life. For me, attending mass on a daily basis has shown all of these things to be true. Living does not necessarily become easier, it becomes more understandable. We come to realize what our path in this life is all about. It is all about God. It is all about what we do on this journey in order to move on to the next world. As I see it, we have only two choices. One is for good and the other is for evil. It is up to us what we choose and if we open our hearts to the Word of God, we will know the difference. Our Lady has come to help us choose through her guidance and through the messages she brings to us from her Son, Jesus.

Three of the visionaries have been given nine of the ten secrets she has promised before the end times come. At that time all of the visionaries will have received ten. Mirjana, who was the first to have been given all of them, has also been chosen to be the one who will release the secrets to the world. This is to happen when the end is at hand. At the direction of Our Holy Mother, Mirjana chose a priest, Franciscan Father Petar Ljubicic to whom she will reveal all the secrets ten days in advance of each one coming to fruition. After Mirjana and Father Ljubicic pray and fast for ten days, he will announce to the world each secret and its meaning three days before each occurs. One thing that I would like to mention at this time is that there will be time after a Permanent sign appears for conversion. The one secret that has been partially revealed regards a sign which the entire world will recognize as having come from God. What it is, we do not know.

Mirjana has said that the entire world will not convert because that would be impossible, but that God wants all of his children to be given time to see, to learn and to hear His Word. We should all know by now that satan did ask God for a century in which to reign over mankind. We are currently living in that century and if you are not aware that satan has been in our midst, you have not been paying attention to what is happening or you do not read Holy Scripture. The time is coming very close to when the world will see the Permanent Sign, which Our Lady says is for the benefit of atheists, or in other words, for those who do not know God. The Permanent Sign will be seen over Apparition Hill, on which she first appeared, for the entire world to witness. At that time, all mankind will know the coming of God in all of His Glory and Majesty.

My husband, Nate and I have been blessed to have seen many signs in Medjugorje since we began our pilgrimages in 2006. Each year, except for my first, when I traveled alone, we have had the honor to be in attendance for Our Mother's visit to Mirjana on October 2nd. Not only have we had the privilege of seeing many wonders on our own, we have been told of miracles of spiritual and physical healing. Many of the accounts have left us with wonder and gratitude in our souls for the gifts of our Heavenly Father. Many of us take them for granted when we read of the miracles in the Bible. And yet, when we talk about them as they happen today, we are sometimes met with blank stares and we often feel disapproval and distain. And yet, each of us, as we recognize that we are children of God, is responsible to spread the gospels of today. This book has its foundation in my need to share with others the gifts that God has for all.

As I wrote previously, each visionary was given the responsibility of praying for special souls. Maria, the souls in purgatory, Ivan, for priests and young people, Vicka and Jacov, the sick and dying, Ivanka, for families, and Mirjana, for non believers. These prayers are part of the many fruits of Medjugorje. I feel that the events, as they occur in that part of the world, are intended to change the entire world. I also feel that the soul of each and every person who goes will be changed if his or her pilgrimage is taken with an open heart to the signs that are Medjugorje.

I wish I could scoop up everyone, who has not been there, and put them down in the courtyard of the Church of St. James. It took years to happen, but my life changed dramatically once I had the experience of being in that world so far from my home. I have been able to accept the fact that I went at the invitation of Our Mother. That alone was difficult for me to grasp but the push was so great that I could not resist. I could have never guessed how astounding the impact of listening to the call would be. For example, how could I have ever known that someday I would write this book. I have been writing all of my life, but where did the courage come from to take on such a huge endeavor. I have struggled within myself many times as I felt I probably could not bring forth the words. However, I do know that Holy Spirit has always been at my side during every moment that I sit at my keyboard. Sometimes it is hard for me to discern from whom the words are coming.

I know that I must tell you that someday soon we will all be living our usual lives, just as we were before September 11, 2001 and we will begin to realize that the final days are upon us. There will be people driving to or from work. They will be getting the kids to school or soccer, having lunch with friends, shopping at the mall or picking up groceries. People will be teaching or nursing. Some will be on business trips away from home and others will be at the office in town. There will be those in hospitals doing or having surgery, others will be on vacation or visiting the family for the first time in years. People will be doing the laundry or putting gas in the car. Then there will be those women who will be giving birth and others having abortions at the same time.

For many it will mean utter confusion and fear much as it was on 9/11. But for those of us who read the Bible, it will mean even more. It might mean that we should have prepared for what is to come. It has not happened yet, so exactly what does preparation mean for you and your loved ones? In my case, it will not be having extra containers of water, cans of food on storage shelves, a camp stove, candles, large boxes of matches, extra dog food or many boxes of laundry detergent and Kleenex. I understand that we should always be prepared for emergencies, but this will be different. To have survival equipment and food supplies is necessary and good because we must be ready to help ourselves and others at all times especially when we face natural disasters. This will not be a natural disaster as we know them. It will be very different. Are you ready?

For all of us who pay attention to the Scriptures and listen to the Messages of Medjugorje, it will mean having oil for our lamps and being ready when the Bridegroom comes as we have read in The Parable of the Ten Virgins. Which of the virgins will you be? Will you squander your lamp oil while you sleep? Will you be able to trim your lamp when the Bridegroom comes? Will Christ recognize you? Do you know Him? Ask yourself, will you be ready for the second coming of Our Savior? Do you know what you need to do to be ready? His Mother, our Mother, is trying to tell us how to prepare. We need to listen to her words. She is not coming on her own. She is being sent by God and she is bringing His messages to us.

"Dear Children,

God wants to save you and sends you messages through people, nature and many things which can only help you to understand that you must change the direction of your life. Thank you for responding to my call."

Message: March 12, 2012

4

THE BOOK

I HEARD A SMALL voice at four in the morning on Tuesday, October 11, 2011. The Holy Spirit said it was time for me to begin writing in earnest. The phones did not ring, and the TV was silent. I could write in peace and so I did, sometimes overwhelmed by memories that needed to be recorded. On our most recent trip to Croatia, my husband Nate and I heard that in the month of August, 2011, four million people visited the tiny village of Medjugorje in Bosnia-Hertcegovina. On Sunday, October 2, 2011, our pilgrimage group stood with an estimated 10,000 people from all over the world, below the Blue Cross at the foot of Apparition Hill, to witness the appearance of The Holy Mother of God to Marjana. On that day, we were to be given a message relayed to us through her from Our Mother. Mary was appearing to Marjana, as she always does on the second day of each month, in order to lead the world to salvation through the messages of love, peace and guidance from her Son, Our Savior Jesus Christ.

I continued to ask myself why I felt the pull to write this book. It was so strong. It was the same pull that I had to go as a pilgrim to Medjugorje each and every time I went. If Our Holy Mother wants you, she beckons and you go. It is the same with the Holy Spirit. There is no denying either of them. Why are they calling us? Because, our world is being destroyed and we need to change our sinful ways. You may have noticed that the end times appear to be very near. I mentioned that before. We do not know when they will come and I am not suggesting that we do. There may have been a lot of devout people in earlier times, who felt that way too, but they are gone and the world is still here. Only God knows when the final days will come, but they look imminent to me. There are so many signs these days. So, I realize that it is time for this book to be written. The world needs the messages of Medjugorje now. Our lives need to change now. We need to live God's messages now. Tomorrow may be no more.

Our Holy Mother has also come for another good reason and just watching the news on television confirms that. God is rapidly being shut out of our world and our lives. Each day we are bombarded with the most horrendous of sins. Satan stalks us, there is no denying that. We are immersed in the murder of babies, not fetuses as some would like to call them. I guess we think of a fetus as something less than human and it makes it easier to ignore this modern day holocaust. Calling a child a fetus makes the crime more palatable I suppose, but there is no denying that a baby is a baby is a baby. And we kill them daily with wholesale abortion, even when they could live outside the womb. What have we become, butchers?

Wars, pornography, child abuse, hatred, anger, cruelty, rape, killings, threats of nuclear destruction, the end of marriage as God intended it to be and the loss of our religious freedoms are what we are facing in our daily lives. The Catholic Church is confronted with the probability of having to close its hospitals in two years because Obama Care mandates that employee insurance must cover the cost of contraception and beyond. Wake up people. The holocaust of WWII came about because people accepted the lies told by their leaders. Our leaders lie. Our current government is telling us that our church has no choice but to provide this coverage even though it goes against our beliefs. This mandate violates the rights of the church with respect to the First Amendment. Many Catholic institutions are suing our government because our rights are being violated. We are being told that what is happening today in our government is for the good of all. We will have the freedom to live off the government and the rich will support us through taxation. This is what our children and grandchildren are being spoon fed and this is the world they will inherit unless we change our lives and follow God. I feel a need to tell you this in case you are not aware of what is going on in our country and in our world. Since I have received the gift of having been called to Medjugorje, I have also been given the responsibility to warn others of the work of satan, which is being carried out by people who wish to lead us down a destructive path. I have had enough of the likes of the left, and the Godless.

For the first time in the history of our nation, we experienced major enemy warfare on our soil on 9/11. God has been kicked down the road and mankind no longer believes in sin. We are living what we have been learning about for years from Scripture. There seems to be no end to natural disasters. We have had earthquakes, floods, forest fires, famines, tornadoes and hurricanes for centuries. Now these disasters are more plentiful and much bigger. We are having tsunamis. They are not new. I knew they existed, but I did not even know just how devastating they were until a short time ago. Interestingly, we have experienced two of them in just a split second in time.

Because of all of these natural disasters millions of people are hungry and homeless. Adding to that, the entire world economy is now in crisis. Wars are breaking out in many countries. Syria is massacring its own people and Israel is being threatened with annihilation by Iran. Iran wants to destroy the entire western world. I believe that God has had enough. Satan is about to see the end of his reign. I suspect that many of us will be part of it. The sins of mankind have brought about this destruction. Our Holy Mother is coming as a messenger from her Son, Jesus Christ, to warn us to stop our sinning, but it does not appear that anyone is listening.

I am writing this book to share the Medjugorje messages with you and ask all the people of this country to stand up for God. We could start by celebrating Christmas for what it is, the birthday of our Savior, Jesus Christ, the Son of God. I am so sick of seeing Christmas cards emblazoned with the words happy holidays. I don't buy them. Or, and this is one of my favorites, now we decorate" holiday trees". The word Christmas is all but extinct. If you want to wish your Jewish friends a Happy Hanukah, send them a Happy Hanukah card. The same should apply to your Muslim friends on their holidays; send them an appropriate card. Do the same for everyone who celebrates Chinese New Year. What is this one size fits all Christmas card? It looks like Christ's birthday has been tossed into a holiday heap. Christmas used to be Holy Day.

Back in the late 80's I was watching a Christmas parade in Los Altos, California. A float depicting the manger scene went by and a little girl, who was standing in front of me, asked her mother what it meant. The mother waved off her child with the words, "Oh that is what Christmas used to be about". I have never forgotten those words and I never will. God have mercy on us, please! We must turn back to our Christian faith. We must stop the crime of abortion. We must honor the sacrament of marriage for what it is, a union between a man and a woman. Notice, I did not say we should, the operative word is must. It would also be nice if people actually started to get married again.

When I look back upon my childhood, I know for certain that I really liked having a mother and father who were married. I had one mom and one dad. I did not have two mothers or two fathers. I don't think I would have enjoyed that. With a family consisting of a mom and a dad, each parent has something different to contribute to the growth, health and morality of a child. God is the one who assembled the family in this manner. We must stop making our own rules and begin to live by God's rules. Why, because He says so! I do not remember ever reading anything anywhere that would suggest to me that God wishes us to change his designs for mankind.

Today in Medjugorje, Our Lady is telling us to follow God and to live His plans for us through prayer. She asks that we pray the Rosary every day. She wants us to fast on bread and water on Wednesdays and Fridays. If fasting is not something we can do, then perhaps spending time with the sick or helping out a neighbor in need or volunteering at a soup kitchen could work for you. There are many ways to give of ourselves for the good of others. Catholics can start living better lives by attending mass and receiving the Sacrament of the Holy Eucharist daily. The Holy Mother tells us to confess our sins at least once a month. If we do, the graces we receive give us the strength to live better lives.

We are also being told to teach our children about God before it is too late to save their souls and ours. You can demonstrate the Ten

Commandments in your family by living them yourselves. Children will learn the Ten Commandments very early in their lives through our acts of kindness and love toward them. Teaching the difference between right and wrong is the first step. This is an act of love, did you know that? As they grow older it becomes important to explain to them the parts of the commandments that address the sins of stealing, lying and cheating. Even killing and adultery can be approached much earlier in today's society. With what they learn through television, the internet, the news media and music today, they are bombarded with such things very early in their lives. Children know so much more today than ever before. We all know that.

To neglect teaching God's Word to our children is to deny them eternity with Him. I am always amazed to hear parents say that the children can pick their faith when they grow up. How in the world would the child pick his or her own faith if they know nothing about God? What if we just decided that they could pick out a language when they reached twenty five and never spoke to them before that time? Or perhaps we could tell them that they can decide to choose to study math somewhere down the path in later years. That wouldn't work, would it? They would be lost in the world. Not teaching them about God will not work either. It is the first thing they should learn. Most children want to know about God. They came from Him.

Through the messages of Medjugorje, we are exposed to God and His Truth. Again, the world needs the messages of Medjugorje. Perhaps what we are being asked to do sounds difficult, but living in hell sounds much harder to me. It is my profound hope that not one person reading this book would want eternity in hell for themselves or their children. If you do not believe that, I suggest that you read a book called "My Descent into Death" by Pastor Howard Storm. He was an atheist when he died. He was sent back to earth by Christ. Today he is a Pastor, spreading the word of God.

"Dear Children,

At this time, in a special way, I call you. Pray with the heart little children. You speak and pray little. Read and meditate on Sacred Scripture and may the words written in it be life for you. I encourage and love you so that in God you may find your peace and joy of living. Thank you for having responded to my call."

Message: February 25, 2012

5

THE MESSAGES

SEVERAL YEARS AGO, BEFORE my first trip to Medjugorje, a book that would significantly change my life made its way into my home. It had a strong impact on me. At the time I had no idea how it came to be in my living room and to this day I still do not. At the time, the author of the book was unknown to me but the subject matter was familiar. When I read the book, I was intrigued by the miracle which drove the author to write it since he apparently had no desire to do so. According to the author, whose name is Wayne Weible, the Holy Mother of God spoke to him and said that she wanted him to write her story, the story of Medjugorje, with her help. He knew little or nothing about Mary and at first wanted nothing to do with her or her request. Not only was Wayne not a Catholic, he was not even sure that he believed in God.

For me, the book was so compelling that I knew that I had to meet him, question him and hear his account for myself. How could a person who espoused to be an unbeliever write such an accurate account of the Holy Mother without her guidance. I knew that she really had to be right there with him. I decided that someday I would find a way to meet Wayne. So I prayed for the help of the Holy Spirit. It always works for me and it can work for you too. He is always with us, though so many of us have no realization of this gift. The Holy Spirit was sent by Jesus to be with us on earth after He ascended into Heaven. Jesus told the apostles before He was taken into heaven, "Where I go, you cannot follow me now. If I go not, the Holy Spirit will not come to you, but if I go I will send Him to you." The Holy Spirit did come on Pentecost and stayed with the people of this earth. He is here with us during every moment of our lives to help, guide and direct us. He helped me in my quest to meet Wayne Weible. I had no doubt that He would do just that.

A while after I had been to Medjugorje the first time, I was given the opportunity I wanted. The man who wrote my mysterious book was scheduled to attend a Marian conference in Las Vegas where one of the visionaries was also slated to speak. Out of the blue, a friend called me to say that he had been checking a website and had discovered that Mirjana, one of the first two young women who saw the Virgin on Apparition Hill would be speaking there at the end of the week. I was sure that we would never get tickets, but as miracles would have it, we did.

It was a small private conference and not many people had heard about it. A few days later, there we were, my husband and I, sitting in a room with about eighty five other people listening to Mirjana Soldo present her Medjugorje testimony. We were actually able to listen to some of the messages from our Holy Mother repeated directly to us from Mirjana, one of the young women she had chosen to receive them. Mirjana was beautiful, humble, gracious and kind. We sat quietly as she described the day our Lady appeared to her and the five other visionaries. These were the stories I had heard about and read without any changes or embellishments. I knew they were true.

After Mirjana spoke, we were allowed questions. She was asked about the souvenir shops that line the streets of Medjugorje. Her answer was simple. Her people were starving. I have heard so many people ask the same question. I even get the question when I am asked about Medjugorje. The shops seem to be a bone of contention among pilgrims. If they have not read or have not listened they do not realize that Mirjana's country was decimated after the civil war that tore through the cities and villages. There were no longer any places to work. Businesses had been destroyed. In Mirjana's country there were no jobs. This was not a case of low employment; it was a case of no employment. Most husbands, fathers, sons, brothers, uncles and grandfathers had been killed. The male population was all but gone. Those who survived had to find a way to stay alive.

When Our Lady began her appearances, pilgrims came from all over the world. The pilgrims wanted rosaries, statues, medals and mementos to take home with them. Villagers began to handcraft rosaries made from the pebbles and stones on Apparition Hill. After the war, the pilgrims were still coming and the demand for the religious articles was still great. Stands and shops opened one after another. Our Holy Mother triumphed. Because of the income generated from the sale of these holy articles, mothers were again able to feed their families.

Dear reader, have you ever starved? If you have not, you do not understand. I certainly do not. We might have an opinion of our own as to what people have to do to find a way to provide food for their loved ones. But that does not give us the right to judge or criticize. In desperate situations, people must find ways of earning money. We pray that what they are doing is not sinful and we hope that their plan will not take advantage of others. We do not think that this happens. We should understand that this village is not Lourdes and it is not Fatima. It is different and Our Lady is there today. In the years during which we traveled to Medjugorje, my husband and I, as well as our friends have purchased many beautiful items for many people, who could not travel there themselves. Never once did we judge the way the people earned their living nor did we feel that we were being exploited.

There was a twofold advantage to the sales in Medjugorje. The pilgrims carry these blessed gifts home to their families and families used them to pray. I think more and more people pray today because of the shops in Medjugorje. I feel that Our Holy Mother had a plan and it worked out very well with the help of God.

After Mirjana spoke, we listened to the other guest speakers at the conference. Wayne Weible, the author I had been waiting to meet came forward and began to tell us how his book had come to be. His story made me realize just how amazingly God works. It was beautiful to hear how the word of God and the messages of Our Holy Mother had changed Wayne. According to his testimony, it took him awhile, a long while, to begin to write, but when he did his book reached a large audience and the story of Medjugorje spread throughout the US and eventually throughout the world. Today Wayne has many books circulating around the world. This is what Our Lady wanted when she asked him to do the job.

Wayne brought many copies of his book to sell at the conference. During a break, I stood patiently in line and finally was given an opportunity to speak with him. I purchased eleven copies of "Medjugorje

The Message" to mail to friends and family, and I asked him to autograph every single one of them. Before I left the conference, I purchased five more books, which gave me additional time to speak with him while he signed them. Wayne asked where I was from and I explained that my husband and I lived in St. George, UT. He immediately expressed a strong desire to bring his story to St. George to speak about his experiences in Medjugorje and share his testimony. We mutually agreed upon a time for him to come. Wayne spoke at the Holiday Inn in St. George in March of 2008, a few months after we met. The evening with Wayne was a wonderful success despite all sorts of other community activities planned that night. That was four years ago and people still talk about it. He brought his message to many of those who needed to hear it and they did.

"Dear Children,

In your life you have all experienced light and darkness. God wants everyone to recognize good and evil. I am calling you to the light which you should carry to all people who are in darkness. People who are in darkness daily come into your homes. Dear Children, give them the light. Thank you for responding to my call."

Message: March 14, 1985

6

IT'S A PILGRIMAGE

THE FIRST TIME I heard about Medjugorje was probably when everybody else did; when it happened and when the rest of the world began to read about it. Around 1986, I was at a business seminar in San Diego when I heard two of my colleagues speak about the pilgrimage they had made to Medjugorje sometime within a year or two after the apparitions began. They shared with the group that the trip was very difficult and that living conditions were quite uncomfortable. They had no indoor plumbing, and sanitary conditions were very sparse. They often slept on sofas and floors. But the message was there and, as time went on, pilgrims, thirsty for knowledge of the apparitions descended on this tiny hamlet by the thousands despite the lack of creature comforts. Hotels and pensions had started to be built and many of the people of Medjugorje began to open their homes to guests who arrived in large numbers daily.

Today the pilgrims go by the millions and the messages remain the same. As I said earlier, I continued to go partially because of Wayne Weibel's book, which had mysteriously appeared in my home and also because of stories I heard from my fellow parishioners at church. These people had traveled to Medjugorje during the war years and upon hearing what they had to say, I decided to see for myself. The first time, my husband was not ready to go, so when I felt the time was right, I boarded a flight alone out of Las Vegas, NV and headed for Washington, DC. There I joined a group of thirty or more pilgrims from all over the US. I met up with them, none of whom I knew, at the Dulles International airport in October of 2006 only to arrive in Medjugorje a day and a half later violently ill, preparing for what I was convinced was my imminent death. I knew the initial reason for my journey, so I could not understand why this was happening to me. So, why would I be in such dire straits on my way to meet my holy Mother Mary? I thought perhaps I was meant to leave this earth. That was because so many events during the trip gave me cause to believe that I had come on this journey to die.

Years before, my father was fearful that I would die even before I was born. I don't know much about it, but my mother lost a baby five to seven years before me. Over time I learned in bits and pieces that the beautiful little girl, Mary, had died during the birthing process. Because of this, my father promised St. Rita of the Roses, as he came to know her, that he would consecrate the new infant to the Blessed Mother through her on its day of birth. Remember, in those days parents were not aware of what the family would welcome, a girl or boy child. The day I arrived, I was taken to the Church of St. Augustine in Detroit and presented to St. Rita. Her feast day had been on May 22nd and I came into the world on May 28th. I arrived on earth a scrawny little thing, weighing just five pounds. I was wrinkled and red and topped with a full head of thick black hair that grew out in all directions. I was told that we had Indian blood in the family and I looked very much like a tiny Native American. Of this I am very proud.

I had been deathly ill several times as a child and remembered being told by my mother that the doctor had pronounced me dead from pneumonia at the age of six months. According to my mother, prayer brought me back. That was the start of years of visits to doctors culminating with infantile rheumatoid arthritis, which crippled me for a time. I also contracted rheumatic fever, a disease that left me with a serious heart murmur. I remembered as a young teen, hearing a doctor tell my mother that I would probably be dead by the age of thirty two because of this heart condition. I was now long past thirty two so I assumed that somebody had forgotten to come and get me earlier and they were making up for it now in this distant part of the world.

Memories of those periods of illness flooded back to me. I had no idea what was happening or why. Since I was miserable, I felt even more alone in the midst of this group with whom I was traveling and I was absolutely certain that death was finally catching up with me. Through all of this, my mind went back to what my friend from church, Michelle, who had been to Medjugorje during the worst possible time, had said to me. "Always remember, this is not a vacation, this is a pilgrimage." She also said that the trip would not be fun but it would be beautiful and spiritually healing. (I certainly needed that.) She added that it would be at best difficult and filled with challenges. I thought to myself that I was not planning to have fun, but I wasn't planning to die either.

But, Michelle was right. She was right when she told me that if I persevered, the blessings and graces would abound within me and the spiritual rewards would be great and never ending. The evening before I left, alone, but not the least concerned, I went to church for a special service. Michelle had been there, rosary in hand as she exited the church. I waited for her in the vestibule hoping for a few last words of guidance. I did not know her very well at that time, but we had a mutual interest in the bible and I was learning from her. She is a convert to the faith and has spent years studying the Catholic Catechism and the Bible, thirsting for knowledge of Christ and His word

What I hoped for, as we flew toward that unknown place, was that I would be among the living when I returned to St. George so I could share my experiences with Michelle. I knew that I was not alone in my misery, many pilgrims who had traveled to Medjugorje, especially during the civil war in that region told of discomforts and hardships. But

the draw to the Queen of Peace in Medjugorje, was stronger and more powerful than any suffering they encountered en-route. My friends at church had told me whom to contact to get there, where to stay and a bit of what to expect when I arrived. However, they didn't tell me about any of this. Michelle did and had warned me in a round-about way. Always the practical thinker, I sat in that plane and tried to figure out how my lifeless body would make its way back to St. George, UT to my husband and how much it would cost to get it there.

I am convinced that The Holy Spirit, began to work in me at that time on an all out scale. During the night I spent on the plane I thought about my life. I had been raised a Catholic by devout parents who worked hard and loved God. I tried to do all that was expected of me as I worked my way throughout twelve years of catholic schools, went on to college for an Associate Degree and then spent a short time at the Jesuit University of Detroit. There I studied, of all things, rhetoric, composition and journalism. Who knew I would write a book in my later years. As I looked back over my life as I anticipated my arrival in Medjugorje, I tried to reflect on what had been instrumental in bringing me to this far off place. I had never deliberately missed Sunday mass and I attended daily mass all through my years in primary and high school. My freshman year in high school was spent at the Blessed Sacrament Academy for Girls, which was attached to the Cathedral near my home in Detroit, Michigan. As a freshman at the Academy, I walked around for a year with the letters BS on my beanie. Somebody forgot the "A". Our Mother Superior essentially told us to get used to it. I became attached to that little beanie and saved it for a long time. It kept me humble. The Pastor at the Cathedral back in the fifties was Cardinal Mooney. The Cardinal said mass for us each morning when he was able to do so. Can you imagine having a Cardinal saying mass every day for you? I guess I knew that this was pretty special but it took a long time for the privilege to sink in. I guess you can even get used to a Cardinal.

Years later I had the honor of shaking the hand of Bishop Fulton J. Sheen in Pennsylvania, which is something else I will never forget. His eyes were those of a saint and I had difficulty looking away. The friend who was with me asked what I had seen when I gazed at him. I saw a beautiful deep soul. I now realize what I learned from some of my experiences. God was walking with me from the beginning of my life and was giving me wonderful memories to draw on. I also began to realize that I was a typical cradle Catholic, who had taken my faith for granted from very early on. I believe that Our Holy Mother and St. Rita never left my side.

I started to work by cleaning houses and baby sitting at the age of eleven. I grew up in a home where money, or the lack of it, was always an issue to be dealt with by my parents who were trying to feed, clothe and educate their family on very little. Working was a way to help out financially at home and to prepare to venture out into the world when the time came. I had grown to be pretty independent. I had even lived in a foreign country in South East Asia for a number of years in later life, but, again, for some reason I was not prepared for what I experienced on this trip to Medjugorje. It was unique. Nothing like this had ever happened to me before. Now, looking back, I know that the things I was given were blessings and that even being very ill was a gift from God.

I had been very excited about going to Southeastern Europe because the Detroit neighborhood, in which I grew up, was Croatian, Serbian and Italian. We had a very large community of Polish people there too, but I was not on my way to Poland. My family was French Canadian. We were the only French family around for miles. Nobody in my neighborhood had any idea what a French Canadian was, even though Canada was across the river from downtown Detroit. One thing I did learn while growing up was that I loved everybody's food and so I had set high expectations on my way to Croatia for what I might find served at the dinner table.

Over and over during the trip, I thought back to the evening before I left when Michelle came out of church carrying a rosary that was crystal and gold. Even in the soft lights of the church vestibule, it sparkled brightly and my eyes were instantly drawn to it. Michelle shared with me that her rosary had previously been silver, but that on the night before leaving for Medjugorje years earlier, as she held the beads and prayed, the rosary started to become warm in her hands and then grew hot. As she looked down at it, the silver began to change to a beautiful gold color and then began to gleam under the light of the lamp in the room. I wondered if my rosaries would turn gold. I had taken several old ones with me. The chains between each bead had turned black on most of them. I was embarrassed to have anyone see them, but they had been with me all my life and they were precious to me, especially the one I had used for my First Communion.

When I finally arrived in Medjugorje, I was barely upright. During the first night there I had a conversation with Our Holy Mother. I told her that it would have been a whole lot more convenient for my husband and my children if she had just asked God to leave me in St. George to die. I kept wondering if there was a mortuary in Medjugorje. Better still, I wondered if there was a crematorium. Cremation would make it easier to get me home on the plane. Then I wondered if there would be a problem getting me through security in that condition. I knew that I would not have to put my liquids into a one quart plastic bag. I would be the one quart plastic bag contents. After all, I had not eaten in hours and I was not very big to begin with. I have a habit of finding humor in everything and I found it amusing that I had arrived under such inconvenient circumstances. Everything just seemed so impossible at the time. I just figured that the best thing to do was to let the Holy Spirit continue to lead me as He had up to this time. I had to let go and let God.

On the morning of the first day after I arrived I became a living pilgrim again with the help of God and a miracle. I walked with others through the fields and vineyards on our way to the Church of St. James. We carried and recited our rosaries. I clung to my First Communion rosary and shed a few tears of joy. I will tell you the reason for the tears soon. Our group encountered many pilgrims coming from and going toward the church as we were. Like us, I was sure that they were talking to Our Holy Mother and asking that she intercede with her Beloved Son for us. We asked for mercy for our Godless society, for the ability to love as He loved us, for kindness to dwell in our hearts and to be able to forgive as He forgave

"Dear Children,

Also today I am with you and I am not losing hope that the world will change for the good and that peace will reign in the hearts of men. Joy will begin to reign in the world because you have opened yourselves to my call and to God's love. The Holy Spirit is changing a multitude of those who have said "yes". Therefore, I desire to say to you now. Thank you for having responded to my call."

Message: January 25, 2011

7

IT'S A LONG WAY TO MEDJUGORJE

ON MY WAY TO Medjugorje that first time, I had stopped overnight in Las Vegas. I was scheduled to fly out of there at six in the morning on the last day of September, 2006. My husband insisted that I stay in a nice place and suggested the luxury hotel, the Bellagio. Let me mention that he wants nothing but the best for me and I find it hard to argue with that. I really did want to stay in a place that would be quiet and comfortable since I am not a good sleeper. I relaxed and watched TV in the early evening and retired at nine. Then I lay there in that luxurious room as each hour ticked by. Tick, Tick, Tick! Sleep simply would not come. Maybe I did snooze a little around two but at two thirty the wake-up call sent me flying into the bathroom for a quick in and out shower.

I have never been one to waste even a second when I have to catch a flight. I usually get to the airport very early so I can have plenty of time to prepare to wait another eight hours for a delayed flight that is later cancelled. This time, of course, I had to be there two hours before the flight anyway, so I decided to be there three hours ahead. I did not take time to have any breakfast that morning as I ran through the lobby of the hotel worrying if I would find a cab in Vegas.

If you don't believe that, I have to think that you don't know people like me. ADHD is a permanent fixture in my life with which I have learned to cope. I am also a double A personality type who has lived with dyslexia all her life. Consequently, I wear holes in my itinerary before I get to the airport because I have it in my hands, checking it for days before leaving on a trip. All the way to the airport I double check, triple check and quadruple check to make sure that I have all of my documents, my money, my itinerary and that I am leaving on the correct date. I am a very pitiful traveler. I am either very hysterical most of the time or deadly quiet as I search for something that I already have in my hands or happen to be wearing at the time.

I am searching constantly and I always seem to have my hands full or I am frantic because they are not. I carry jackets when I could be wearing them and I wear shoes with laces which I have difficulty putting back on as I leave the security area. I am good at keeping my liquids to a minimum and then wonder when I get somewhere why I don't have hand lotion with me. As I look around, however, I seem to see a whole lot of other people just like me in the boarding areas. Most people look frantic, panicked or just plain numb. I love the ones who walk around endlessly and then look shocked when they discover they are at the wrong gate and their plane has already left.

The taxi was waiting for me as I cruised through the heavy luxurious gold doors of the elegant Bellagio Casino and Hotel. That was the last that I was to feel well for a long time to come. Immediately as I got into the taxi and asked to be taken to the airport, the driver wanted to know where I was headed. I answered pretty much like this: To a place I am sure you have never heard of in Southeastern Europe, in the former country of Yugoslavia, now known as Croatia. Actually, the name of the place is Medjugorje and it is located in Bosnia-Herzegovina in the mountains above the Adriatic Sea. I have no Idea how I came up with all of that Wikipedia jargon in the middle of the night in my sleep deprived condition. His answer went pretty much like mine. I do not remember his exact answer, but it went something like this: Yeah,

I have heard of it. My mom went there awhile ago and later I made a little St. James church out of toothpicks for her after she came back. She keeps it on the dresser in her bedroom. It hasn't fallen apart yet. It actually looks just like the church in Medjugorje. I would like to go there myself, but I can't afford it on what I make driving a cab. How'd you like the Bellagio? I was stunned. Out of the zillions of cabs in Las Vegas, I got into the taxi of a man who not only knew all about where I was going, but had made his mom a copy of St. James Church out of toothpicks! I wonder if she still has it on her dresser. Where is the Holy Spirit when you need him? Most likely he is sitting right next to you in the cab or wherever you happen to be.

We talked a lot and it turned out that my driver came from New Jersey. He loved the weather in Las Vegas, where he now lived and worked. He was so nice and offered to pray for me as I flew across the world. He asked me to pray for him in Medjugorje. I left the cab wondering if I had just ridden with and conversed with one of my Guardian Angels. Who was this man? Wherever had he come from, I mean really come from? I began my journey blessed to have met him. I hope that he will someday read this book and remember that trip to the airport on the dark early morning at the end of September, 2006.

I actually got out of Las Vegas on a plane that took off on time. I have to admit that I am a bit of a dork, the best description I can come up with, at airports, at any airport. I arrive pulling bags that always flip over, wheels up. I can never find my itinerary, so I carry a book, which I never read. I have it just to hold the tickets or whatever I happen to have with me at that moment. I always worry about putting the book down somewhere, so I add that to the rest of the worries. I tell myself to put all of this into the hands of God, and I do, but I worry anyway. I am a career worrier. I worry about worrying.

I landed at Dulles convinced that I would not find the International Terminal. However, it didn't take me long once I found and followed the tired signs down a long dark corridor, sheathed in plastic. It was obvious that there was a good deal of renovation going on in this part of the airport. Ahead was a large dismal boarding area attached by a hallway leading out of the main terminal. It was nothing to write home about and certainly did not stir up excitement in me in spite of the fact that I was a pilgrim embarking on a flight to Vienna in route to Southeastern Europe where I would hopefully arrive at my destination the next day.

By the time I found the International section of the terminal I was very hungry. I had not had food since the night before, so I started to look for some sort of restaurant or kiosk. I looked ahead as I entered the boarding area and immediately found myself surrounded by my fellow pilgrims all wearing identification tags from "206 Tours", the group I had signed up with. Of course, I had not worn my tag. I have an aversion to things hanging around my neck or plastered to my clothes that announce "Hi, My name is Rita". I despise tags. The group guessed that I was one of them and suggested that I find my ID. I was hugged and welcomed and then they all went back to the conversations they were having prior to my arrival. I stood there trying to figure out where I could find food. By then, I was really starving and the only place that appeared to have anything I could eat was a small hole in the wall stand with a worn out looking man selling those awful sandwiches that were probably prepared in China a week before. I bought a tuna on wheat. It was dry and hard, and the lettuce was limp. I took the lettuce out and threw it away. I ate what I could, which was not much. I then walked back to where my group stood talking. As I looked around, I noticed somebody in the crowd who looked to be pretty much as lost as I felt and walked up to her. It appeared to me that she knew some of the people. I found out later that she did know someone through her work with a cosmetic company. I said hi to her and introduced myself.

She said, "Hi, my name is Nina".

"Especially little children, pray for the gifts of the Holy Spirit so that in the spirit of love every day and in every situation, you may be closer to your fellow-man; and that in wisdom and love you may overcome every difficulty. Thank you for having responded to my call."

Message: May 25, 2000

8

THE GIFT

I HAVE HEARD IT said that a pilgrim experiences many miracles the first time he or she visits Medjugorje, but, as usual, I was not prepared for what would happen next. Nina was to become my constant companion for the following ten days. We guided each other, we laughed, we ran for the front seat on the busses and the best spot in the choir loft at the St. James church in Medjugorje. We were always the first in the church, lining up way before anyone else got there. We cried on each other's shoulders and shared all of our experiences. At one point, Nina kept me from being tossed off Cross Mountain by a stampeding enthusiastic crowd of Italian pilgrims. She does not remember that, but I do. We were half way down the mountain and Nina was about 30 feet behind me. Suddenly I heard her scream, "Rita, grab a tree". I figured I would do as she said and ask questions later. I clung to a relatively mature tree as what seemed like all of Italy rained down on me at a gallop, laughing, talking and singing, and hardly aware of my presence.

When the dust settled, I looked down at my feet and noticed that I was on the edge of the mountain looking down at a very long drop. I think Nina saved my life that day. This is something I will never forget whenever I think about that first trip to Medjugorje. Nina and I were the most kindred of souls despite the fact that I was at least twenty years older than she. Nina was a gift from God and I will always be most grateful to have known her. We had a glorious time together, one which I will always remember. But I digress.

That limp sandwich had not done much to quell the grumbling and the discomfort of my poor stomach, besides one bite of that potential poison was about all I could tolerate. The plane ride was also less than comfortable by a long shot. We flew over the ocean at night, but nobody slept. Instead, they talked and laughed in excitement. The lights in the cabin were on and bright for most of the duration of the trip. As I mentioned, I had not slept much at the hotel either. The crew served dinner right after we boarded the aircraft and, once again, I was not able to eat much of anything. I have digestive intolerances which include the inability to eat butter (not cheese, not milk, not margarine, only butter), and, sadly, chocolate, which can send me directly to the nearest hospital. So, I have to be careful about what I consume. Incredible as it sounds being allergic to chocolate has an upside. It is one of God's blessings. I have stayed thin.

Alcohol can send me to the hospital with wretched migraines. Alcohol is something that rarely concerns me because it is not in food as much as chocolate or butter. The food on the flight was full of butter, so I had one or two hard dry rolls and some water to wash them down. Desert was a large soft chocolate chip cookie, so I gave it away and hoped to find some "Rita Kosher Food" at our destination. By the time we arrived in Vienna, I had not eaten much or slept for at least two days.

We entered the terminal in Vienna only to find the boarding area packed to the gunnels with passengers whose flights had either been delayed or cancelled. There was a group of traditional Hasidic Jewish pilgrims headed to the Holy Land. The men wore their hair in pigtails which fell on each side of their bearded chins. They also wore small black fedoras. For the most part, the women were dressed in long voluminous skirts with full sleeved tops. Men and women both toted children in their arms or held their hands as they walked beside their parents. The children were beautiful and well behaved under very difficult circumstances. These people had arrived shortly after us and were told that their flight out had been cancelled and there was no replacement in route. They scurried about wearing concerned expressions as they attempted to get help which did not appear to come.

The boarding area was mobbed and finding a restaurant was impossible. Everything was chaotic and frantic. There were few seats to begin with and when one became vacant, twenty people went diving for it, leaving behind some very hostile and tired people, who were still standing. We finally did get into the only small eating area. I just drank coffee because the only rolls were croissants which, of course, are full of butter. I finally managed to get a shallow bowl of soup as the day wore on. It had little positive impact on my growing sickness which was beginning to seriously rear its ugly head.

The waiting area was hot, crowded and uncomfortable. We were constantly herded from one line to another, often finding that we were in the wrong one. Our estimated time of departure to Dubrovnik in Croatia was eight hours. It took about ten, and we stood a great deal of the time. We walked around the only gift shop looking for snacks. It appeared to me that all of them seemed to be made of chocolate. Every cookie in the place was either made of solid chocolate or covered with chocolate or dotted with chocolate or layered with chocolate. I fully expected to see chocolate covered ants.

Most of us carried only US dollars which were not welcomed as I recall. When we used plastic, we had to produce our passports as identification. I was pretty proud of myself because I was not buying any of the chocolate treats that lined the cases, the shelves and the racks in the gift shop until I decided it would be nice to get some as Christmas gifts. Eventually, I had to produce my passport and then every fifteen minutes thereafter, I worried and wondered if I had returned it to its proper place in the pouch which hung around my neck for the sake of safety.

The lines everywhere in the airport were long and the people were testy to say the least. A group of us finally spotted a place where there were available seats only to discover that it was a smoking lounge. I lasted about thirty seconds in there and decided to spend the next five hours walking around and standing in the terminal. The airport in Vienna seemed to me to be a bit grim at that time and it was not one to which I was eager to return. We finally boarded a flight to our final destination and arrived in Dubrovnik very late to be greeted by our newest best friend, Nevis, our tour guide for the days to come.

"Dear Children,

Today I call you in a special way to become open to God and for each of your hearts today to become a place of Jesus' birth. Little children, throughout all of this time that God permits me to be with you, I desire to lead you to the joy of your life. Little children, the only true joy of your life is God. Therefore, dear children, do not seek joy in the things of this earth, but open your hearts and accept God. Little children, everything passes, only God remains in your heart. Thank you for having responded to my call."

Message: December 25, 2007

9

ROCKS AND ROLLS

WHEN WE BOARDED THE bus for the three hour trip to Medjugorje along the shore line and through the mountains, all was well. I was actually feeling fairly human at this point. I had slept for about an hour on the flight between Vienna and Dubrovnik. We were all grateful to be on the ground and on our way. The excitement was contagious. Nina and I grabbed the first seat up front behind the driver. Once we discovered how nice the front seat was, we were the first ones on the bus all the time, just like two eager little girls. We had the best view as we wound our way past stunning vistas of the Adriatic Sea, where the waters ran from turquoise to a deep emerald blue green with the bright sun glinting upon soft undulating waves. I was overcome by the exquisite beauty surrounding me. I felt like I was headed toward heaven. In retrospect, I guess I was. What a magnificent countryside. We drove past little white houses with roofs of faded red tiles. Everything was clean.

There were rocks everywhere dotting the rolling fields and mountains. I felt alive and vibrant despite the lack of food and sleep and then suddenly things changed and I began to hit a wall. We pulled into a rest stop. Others left the bus to use the facilities and get water. My head began to pound. I became extremely dizzy as I attempted to go down the steps of the bus to the outdoors. I could hardly stand. I got back on the bus feeling extreme nausea and I spent the next part of the journey trying to control my insides to keep them from tossing up everything I had eaten in the past thirty years of my life.

As we rode the bus to Medjugorje from Dubrovnik, Nevis kept telling us that we would be served a wonderful meal by our hostess, Yelka, once we reached our final destination. Every time she mentioned food, my insides revolted and threatened to rebel momentarily. Hours later we arrived in the neighborhood which we were to call home for the next ten days. It was late and dark outside by then. I begged to be let off of the bus so I could find a field in which to lie down and die. Fortunately, the bus halted in front of the home of the visionary, Ivan and not the field next door. Nevis helped me down from the bus. I was given a key and a nice man took me to my room on the second floor.

Later, I decided that the person who led me to my room was Michael the Archangel. He was big, strong and brought up my luggage. To me he was very special. I have found in the years that I have gone there that Medjugorje is full of saints like that. Actually, he was a nice man who appeared to have a great deal of compassion for me considering my circumstances. I had no idea who he was, but I thanked him as best I could and as quickly as possible because as he left, a storm began to rage in my body. I now know who he is. And, he is special. He is the man who interprets for Mirjana. We met Mickey in Vegas, I should have thanked him. Michael? Mickey? I was right!

I collapsed and could no longer stay on my feet. My legs were like rubber bands. I found myself slithering around on the floor in my room from the bed to bathroom where I expelled every evil lurking in my furious intestines. By now, I was so weak that I could barely move. Several times I gave into my miserable condition and slept intermittently on the floor until the sun came up. I had no idea what was happening to me or why. I had not eaten or slept in hours, but I had done that before and never had such brutal consequences as a result. I learned later that this was all a part of a purge; emotionally, physically and spiritually. I needed food. Somehow I managed to find a piece of paper in my possessions. I tore it off of my itinerary and wrote the words "help me" on it before

I passed it under the door of my room. People who were also staying at Ivan's with me saw the note and knocked on the door. I asked for toast. About an hour later, a hard dry chunk of bread arrived by another angel. I thought perhaps it was Nevis. At the time I had no idea who it was, but I did learn years later that a dear lady named Mary was aware of my circumstances and was moved to help. On this trip, Mary became a part of the team of Nina and Rita and we spent wonderful hours exploring Medjugorje and praying together as we made our way through paths, hills and mountains.

I took the toast and began to consume it slowly. I could not bite into it because it was pretty much like a piece of petrified wood. I remembered that during the night I had chided the Holy Mother for bringing me to the other side of the world in this miserable condition. I told her that my husband would have difficulty transporting my body back to the states and that it would be a very costly task. Again, I pondered where and how he could find a crematory in this small mountain village.

Moments later I began to feel strength surge into my body. I had been praying as I managed to get bites of bread down. Miraculously and suddenly I stood up and went to the window in the corner of the room to look out on the lovely garden below. As I stood there I recited the Hail Mary holding my First Communion rosary in my hands. I looked down at it as it began to be transformed from one with dark and blackened chains to a beautiful rosary that gleamed gold in the morning rays of the sun. I could not believe that the sea of violence that convulsed my entire being the night before was over and that now I stood watching a miracle take place before my eyes.

I hurried to shower and dress and then ran down the stairs and out into a glorious day to walk to the home where most of my new pilgrim friends were gathered. I found the house, remembering the instructions given to me by Nevis the night before when I was dropped off. Finding the house was another miracle, since my brain had been unable to function at all just an hour or so earlier. The yellow house was at the end of the road and I entered. I was greeted as another Lazarus returning from the dead. Before I left the house of Ivan, I made sure I had my miracle rosary with me so that I could carry it with me all day.

"Dear Children,

May this time for you be a time of prayer. Rest your body and spirit. May they be in God's love. Permit me little children to lead you. Open your hearts to the Holy Spirit so that all the good that is in you may blossom and bear fruit one hundred fold. Begin and end the day with prayer with the heart. Thank you for having responded to my call."

Message: July 25, 2011

10

JUST LIKE HOME

OUR HOSTESS, YELKA, TURNED out to be a lovely and sweet young woman. She cooked foods that I remembered and loved as a child growing up in my ethnic neighborhood in Detroit. Yelka's meals were beyond delicious. The rooms were squeaky clean. The home was cheerful and I was surrounded by people who were there for the same reason that I was. Breakfast was served to me and life surged back into my body and soul. Nina seemed happy to see me as we went off to begin our pilgrimage together with other eager pilgrims. I remember that I got to the house just in time to join the walk through the vineyards and fields which ended on a short paved path lined with shops. We saw people vending their wares as we walked. Dogs and cats wandered right beside us along the way. At the end of our short journey, we entered an enclosed walkway. It opened onto the campus of the church, which stood there like a beacon of faith. The doors were open as we approached that morning welcoming us into the house of God. We entered and were immediately wrapped in the loving arms of our Savior as well as many of His flock.

I have to be honest here. We were filtering into a very large crowd of people all crammed into a small space. As we approached the side door of the church with the other pilgrims, each of us was trying to jockey ourselves into the closest position to enter first and run ahead of everyone else for a good seat. The description of a good seat in this case is an oxymoron if there ever was one. If you did get a seat, any seat, so did twenty other people. Actually they were all "good" seats if you got one. We were stuffed into pews as tightly filled as the pants of a three hundred pound man wearing size two jeans. The first thought that crossed my mind was that our fire department at home would be emptying the church like a hungry person diving into a small bag of peanuts on a long flight across the pond. There is no way we would be allowed to hear mass under such crowded conditions in the US.

The church is always filled way beyond capacity. I have no idea how many people can be seated appropriately, but then, that never happens anyway, so it is of no consequence. There are always double or triple the number of people for seats available. Crowds fill the center aisle or sit on the floor at the bottom of the altar. If a pew holds twelve people, you will find sixteen jammed in the space. If you worry about something catching on fire and being caught in a frenzy trying to exit the church, don't. Just put your trust in Jesus and follow the mass.

That is exactly what I did as the beautiful celebration got under way. I forgot about turning into a piece of toast and joined in the liturgy and the music. I marveled at the thirty or more priests concelebrating the mass. I was astonished as I watched all of them come down off the altar carrying chalices and going throughout the church distributing communion to the hundreds of outstretched hands lining the aisles. Those who were not handing out the hosts inside the church were going to the side courtyards where there were probably thousands of the faithful listening to the mass on loudspeakers.

In addition to the courtyards on each side of the church, there are rows of seats that can accommodate up to five thousand people behind the church. Each evening an International mass is celebrated at six pm at the outdoor altar. Pilgrims are provided radios which broadcast the mass in many different languages. That way we can all understand what is being said. The seating area is always overflowing. Because of this, many people end up sitting on the grass behind it. I understand that the evening outdoor mass is said daily from early March through the end of October, when the north winds begin to blow.

After the mass was over the first day, we all filed out into the plaza in front of the church to meet with Nevis. Each day, she had every hour and minute planned for us. There is so much to see and touch and feel in Medjugorje, however, some of what happens is not always on the agenda. A few days into the trip, we had the pleasure of celebrating with Father Jim White, our pilgrim priest, the 25th anniversary of his ordination. Father White is a wonderful man and we all grew to love him very early on. We were not prepared for the celebration, especially not Father. It was a nice surprise for him. However, Nives had arranged to have him celebrate the mass at St. James on the morning of his anniversary. He was aware of that.

Our group was invited to sit in the choir area to lead the hymns. Nina and I got to church long before anyone else. We wanted the very best seat with a view of the altar. That was not to be. The best seat did not necessarily guarantee the best view, so we dashed about like second graders into the choir section and picked out what we considered to be the most advantageous location.

We positioned ourselves along the front corner of the rail separating us from the congregation and congratulated ourselves on being the smartest and the fastest. I never had any compunction about doing any of this because there was absolutely nothing in Medjugorje I ever wanted to miss. I felt young and ready to go. The Holy Spirit had poured his breath into my body and soul. There was no other answer for me to have such strength considering my age and the condition I had been in just a short time before. I was quite delighted with my enthusiasm and energy. I felt my faith was being renewed. I was discovering God again as a young catholic would. I was seeing Jesus through the eyes of a child. I was finding an exciting new life in the Holy Spirit.

As the mass progressed, I kept creeping closer and closer to the organ and the microphone. I could hear a wonderful male voice coming from that direction and I decided that I would dearly love to harmonize with whom ever had that glorious talent. As a young person, I had been trained in light opera. I was also blessed with the ability to harmonize naturally. I just had to sing with that man, who had come down from heaven just for the occasion of Father White's Anniversary. Naturally, I assumed that everybody in Medjugorje had come down from above.

I finally managed to get right up beside this brilliant singer and softly, but surely, began to sing in a whisper quietly along with him, at first tentatively and finally boldly. I was so happy. Another miracle was taking place, this time deep in my musical soul. Then it happened. He started to sing the Ave Maria. A hush fell upon the entire congregation as he sang my most beloved hymn. I moved away from the microphone so that I could not be heard and I harmonized quietly with him as tears rolled down my cheeks. Finally, I felt my throat tighten and the sound would not escape my lips. Instead I sang out in my heart and I listened to my voice intertwined with his in my soul. I had no idea who this man was or if I would ever hear his voice again, but I knew that I would never forget that precious moment.

"Dear Children,

With joy, persistently work on your conversion. Offer all your joys and sorrows to my Immaculate Heart that I may lead you all to my most beloved Son, so that you may find joy in His Heart. I am with you to instruct you and to lead you towards eternity. Thank you for having responded to my call."

Message: September 25, 2009

11

MIRACLES

IT IS HARD FOR me to remember the exact things that I experienced during each and every pilgrimage to Medjugorje, but the first trip does stand out in my mind. Everything was new. Each morning, after a beautiful breakfast, we went to the ten o'clock mass at St. James Church. We always prayed together as we walked to the village through the vineyards. After emerging from the mass on the first morning, we followed Nevis to the area behind the church to see the beautiful statue of the Risen Christ. Pilgrims line up to use a small cloth to collect unexplainable drops of a mixture of oil and water which exudes from the leg of Christ. There are times when the weeping is not evident. There is absolutely no scientific explanation for this phenomenon. When the water drips, it takes the appearance of the beads of a rosary. This beautiful bronze statue graces a walkway which leads the pilgrim into the area where are found Mysteries of the Rosary. These mysteries are painted on mosaic tiles and they surround a peaceful area where one can walk slowly while meditating on the lifetime of Christ. Beyond this area, further along the path is a cemetery where the body of Father Slavko Barbaric is interned.

I believe it was on this same day that three of us went back into the village around five thirty in the evening. As we walked along together, almost at the same moment we all turned to the west toward the setting sun and saw one of the most amazing sights that any of us had ever seen in our lives. We saw colors that were not of this world. Purple was not really purple, pink was not pink, green was not green, but a combination of many colors that blended into each other. The only way to explain these incredible hues is to say that they are not of this world. I saw those colors again later in the week during another extraordinary experience I was given. This particular evening however, the sun had come down to earth and looked many, many times larger than any of us had ever seen it. It pulsated, its colors changed from moment to moment and the brilliance of the sun became brighter than any light I had ever seen. It was never difficult to look at the sun, it was only impossible to turn away. Once again, I had witnessed a miracle in Medjugorje and there were many more to come.

We went into the village seeking out others in our group to find out if they had seen the colors and activity of the sun. We had seen pilgrims ahead of us on the road stop and look and point, and we had also seen other people stop, look toward the sun and walk on. We wondered why they had not been as interested in looking as we had. I later grew to understand that not everybody sees everything the same way. Some pilgrims are open and others, for whatever reason, are blind to what is happening around them. Why, I cannot say. I know that there are those who go to Medjugorje for the express purpose of seeing the miracles that they have heard about and come away disappointed and disheartened. And yet, some of the same sort people do see and do experience wonderful things even though they are not there for the right reasons. It is important to go to Medjugorje with no preconceived notions or expectations. It is often said that one sees so much on the first trip that they can hardly contain it all, and yet I have met people who have been there twenty times and have never seen a thing. However, they did feel the presence of Our Holy Mother and came away spiritually renewed and awakened in the Lord. They do not need miracles to sustain their faith or their Christian strength, they only need to believe and trust in the Lord. The most important reason to go to Medjugorje is to experience the love that comes from the apparitions that have occurred for over thirty years.

I was not to witness Mirjana's apparition on my first trip. As I recall and I think I am correct, we all arrived on the morning of the apparition and consequently missed it. So, I will tell you what happened the following year when my husband, Nate, and I were there together. This second year for me and my husband's first year was not a whole lot more comfortable than my first experience. However, this time I did not think I was going to die. Actually, it was a bit amusing from start to finish. I will tell you all about it in a following chapter, but for now, let me tell you about Mirjana's apparition that we were both able to attend.

After arriving very late into Medjugorje the night before and getting to bed at midnight, Nate and I were back up at three am hiking over to a place called Cenacolo, awaiting the arrival of Mirjana, prior to the apparition, which was to begin at nine. Presently she arrived with her husband with her interpreter at her side. As we waited in silence, we pondered what the experience would be like. How does one explain what it is to stand in the presence of God's Mother? I can only say that it was a blessed privilege to be there when Mirjana, who was kneeling before a beautiful altar prepared for the coming of the Holy Mother, lifted her head and began to converse with the Mother of God. Prior to that, silence was requested but there were still whispers throughout the crowd. People had been shifting in their places and there were still many sounds, including those from prayers being said out in the hall. As we watched Marijana from behind, we could feel the penetrating electricity around us. This was to become one moment in time, which my husband and I would never forget. It will always be one of the spiritual highlights of our time here on earth.

Suddenly Mirjana looked up toward heaven and the ecstasy of the moment spread out over all those present. The silence became like a veil wrapping all of us in peace, serenity and God's grace. Without hearing, we knew that Our Lady was conversing with Mirjana. We have read that her voice is like tinkling crystal, delicate and beautiful and not of this world. Our Mother uses the language of the person to whom she is speaking. We all stood very still, not because we were trying to, but because our bodies desired that we do so. Suddenly, as quickly as it had begun, the apparition was over. It took a few moments for Mirjana to come back into our earthly realm. She was escorted out and we ventured quietly into the sunny day. We were told that there were thousands of people standing on the hill outside, above the building where we had been.

As I said, we were at Cenacolo, a community organized by a nun by the name of Sister Elvira. for young men and eventually young women who were lost to drug addiction. There are many Cenacolos throughout the world, with one located in the United States. This one in Medjugorje was and still is a thriving community and has grown tremendously even during the years during which I was privileged to visit. After getting up in the middle of the night, Nate and I entered a hall where hundreds of pilgrims were already in attendance at four in the morning. At that point we still had several hours to wait. At first we were able to sit on the floor but presently sitting became out of the question. We were literally packed in. I could not begin to guess how many were present inside for the apparition of our Holy Mother to Mirjana that day. It was October 2, 2007. The hall was hot and noisy. People were fainting. Trying to move was not even a consideration. I always felt that we both remained standing because of the crush of all the people around us. However, in spite of the discomfort, we were happy to be there and we will always be grateful for that morning in our lives.

We did see Our Mother and we not hear the words that she spoke to Mirjana; one, of course, never does, but we felt her presence and a feeling of love spread out over all of us. When we exited the hall into the sunshine, I had a feeling of overwhelming joy. I was not at all tired even though I had been up all night. I also felt peace. I always felt peace in Medjugorje. That feeling began with the first morning of my first trip to this blessed place when my rosary turned gold in the sunshine at the window. I feel it every time I step off the bus and my feet touch the hallowed ground.

"Dear Children,

Also today I bring you my blessing. I bless you all and I call you to grow on this way, which God has begun through me for your salvation. Pray, fast and joyfully witness your faith, little children, and may your heart always be filled with prayer. Thank you for having responded to my call."

Message: October 25, 2009

12

SAINTS OF THE MOUNTAINS

AT THE BEGINNING OF this book I spoke of having gone to Seroki-Brigij. The first time I went there, Father White concelebrated mass with Father Jozo. I met Nancy Lotta there that day. She was the interpreter for Father Jozo and I stood and talked with her after the mass. Nancy is a beautiful, soft spoken woman with a serene manner. I was taken by her quiet, gentle voice and I was drawn to her immediately as someone I would like to know. At this juncture in my journey, I felt as though I might be walking in heaven and that everyone around me was a saint. It was beyond anything I had ever experienced before in my life and I began to feel a distinct change taking place in my heart and soul. I felt filled with The Holy Spirit but unable to communicate my feelings to anyone. I began to withdraw into myself as I had never done before. The feeling was both exhilarating and calming for me, quite a contrast. Nancy and her husband Patrick live at a place known to our pilgrim group as "The Castle". It is one of my very favorite places in Medjugorje.

Those of us, who were fledgling Pilgrims, were beginning to find our way around Medjugorje. We enjoyed walking to mass in the morning through the vineyards. One of the first places that Nevis took us to was Apparition Hill. I don't think any of us were prepared for the rocks that we encountered as we climbed to the top past the beautiful depictions of the decades of the rosary. It was a special honor to be chosen to lead the group in prayer and to hear all of the voices lifted to heaven, realizing that the children had done the very same thing at the request of the Mother of God. For me the experience was so moving as to bring tears to my eyes. I went from decade to decade in awe of where I was, what I was experiencing and knowing that my heavenly mother had appeared on this mountain where I now stood and prayed.

I looked out over the valley toward the church of St. James, searching for the location of our home in the village and wondering what was ahead for me as time went on. I had seen a very old, very black and very tarnished rosary turn to gold in my hands, right before my eyes. I was certain at one moment that I was dying and then felt twenty years younger the next. I had climbed the hill where the miracles of Medjugorje had all begun and felt joy fill my heart to the point where I was sure it would burst. I was overwhelmed, but I was still not ready for what would happen next.

I am not sure exactly which day we went to the castle. But I do remember, for that matter, that I had no idea what the castle was or where it was. I had no idea why we were going either. I could not even imagine what a castle was doing in Medjugorje. However, I was aware that this part of the world had been full of castles in the distant past. Perhaps the castle was something left from an earlier time, that it was a ruin. I knew little about Croatia and had never expected to go there. At the time of my visit, I certainly knew nothing about its history. I thought a lot about the castle and I can honestly say that it certainly did not turn out to be what I had expected.

On the morning of our visit, our group followed Nevis out of Yelka's driveway, turned right and went down the road a short distance. We turned right again to cut through a newly plowed plot of land. The first thing I noticed was that an older gentleman was sitting next to what looked to me like a still in the Ozarks back home in West Virginia. For those of you who do not know what a "still" is, I will explain. It is an apparatus or stove used for distilling "Moonshine" for consumption. Moonshine is a very strong alcoholic beverage that got its start in the

Ozarks in the US. Before that it probably came over from Scotland or Ireland with the people who settled in hills of Appalachia. I had never actually seen a real still in the area, even though I had traveled through those mountains in West Virginia many years before. It certainly had the look of a still from photos I had seen.

The man I saw was tending a fire under this "stove". I could see smoke coming out of the top. The man was sitting next to it tending the fire and smoking a cigarette. I had no idea who he was, but I was pretty sure that what he was doing might not be legal, at least in my world. I did find out a short time later that the man was Yelka's father. He was indeed tending a still and producing "white lightening". It is not illegal to sell his alcohol in Croatia. That same dear man, whom Nate and I learned to know and love in the coming years, also handcrafted beautiful rosaries made of the stone from Apparition Hill. It is interesting to note that pilgrims bought both the white lightening and the rosaries from Marko, which is his name. He had a thriving business going in his little corner of the world and the pilgrims were more than happy to keep it alive and doing well.

As we walked on, we came to open land where I spotted goats. I am an animal lover so my first inclination was to go over to pet them but I didn't. Everything in Medjugorje looks peaceful, but I was not sure about how peaceful the goats might be. I kept my head down so that I could watch where I was stepping. I just followed along with the group until we eventually came to a high wooden gate. Nevis approached the gate and knocked, calling out to Patrick, the owner of the castle, to no avail. Patrick did not respond. This went on for a few minutes and then, thanks to modern technology, she whipped out her cell phone and began to dial. Within minutes Sir Patrick of the Castle stood holding the gate open to admit us inside the stone walls of one of the most amazing and interesting construction sites I had ever seen.

All around us were moats and towers and beautiful gardens. Some were still under construction. We watched as a very thin young man carried and installed a beautiful white stone statue of Mary in a new garden. The statue appeared to be bigger and heavier than he was, but he did not seem to care. He lovingly set the statue down and made the Sign of the Cross as he knelt on the ground to honor Our Holy Mother. A short time later, I noticed him planting little rose bushes around the statue. As we continued our tour, we saw meeting rooms in buildings that looked as though King Arthur might be holding court inside at a round table. At the end of a stone path there stood a small lovely and peaceful chapel. I could not believe what I was seeing and I still cannot fathom how this could have happened in the middle of what seemed to me to be nowhere.

I was very surprised to see Nancy there, the same woman I had met when we visited Father Jozo. She was the Nancy of the soft voice and kindly manner. I immediately went to her and announced that she and I had just met a day or so before and that I was privileged and honored to see her again I was to encounter Nancy again on Cross Mountain a day or two later. Each time we met, she greeted me as a dear friend. She still does. Each and every time I am in Medjugorje, she continues to hold a special place in my heart as one of the most saintly people I have ever met. By the way, Nancy makes up in part for the fact that David Parke, whom I have met a number of times, has no idea who I am or where I come from. I am sure you are wondering who in the world David happens to be. I will tell you all about him in detail later.

Nancy and her husband Patrick built the castle. The castle is dedicated to the Holy Mother and it is often used to house priests who come to Medjugorje from all over the world for retreats. This year a church is in the stages of being built on the grounds. I noticed when we were last there, that the little rosebushes planted by the thin young man at the feet of the statue of the Holy Mother have grown. They are beautiful and fragrant and I am sure that she loves having them there.

The story of Nancy and Patrick is a long and beautiful one. I wish I could share it with you, but I will not, because only Patrick and Nancy should do that. It is an amazing story of miracles. The castle plays an important part in one of my personal miracle stories of Medjugorje. Suffice it to say that it is a story of conversion as no other and I often think of it when I dream of my next trip there which begins the day I return home from my previous one. I am never far from Medjugorje in my heart and I know that it is the closest thing to heaven on earth, which I can prove with the help of the little boy Jacov.

When we left the castle that sunny day after hearing Patrick share his testimony of conversion, I was walking on and in the clouds. This may have contributed to my confusion about what happened to me next. Every day presented another miracle, but this was early in the game and there seemed to be no end to the unbelievable events that I was experiencing even then. There were perhaps six or eight of us in our group as we started to return to Yelka's. I was not really entering into the conversation at the time because I was so wrapped up in the story that Patrick had just shared with us about how he and Nancy came to be in Medjugorje. I had lingered behind my fellow pilgrims to have a word or two with Patrick before leaving. He was very kind and listened as I spoke from my heart to him. I told him that I had fallen in love with this beautiful country and shared the fact that if we did not have children, grandchildren and animals back in the US, I would attempt to pull up stakes and spend the rest of my life with my husband exactly where he and I stood at that moment.

Patrick told me to go home, get my Nate and come back immediately to settle in. His words were, "We can have a Bar-B-Q". Wouldn't it be great, I thought, living in this heavenly place, surrounded by peace and having Bar-B-Qs with Nancy and Patrick. I am sure that Patrick invites everybody to move to Medjugorje to have Bar-B-Qs with the two of them. I probably was dreaming about that as I walked a few feet behind my group back through the field from which we had come. Suddenly everything around me changed.

I had been watching the ground for ruts and little goat deposits when I felt a need to look up at the sky. I saw a silvery, diaphanous curtain open before me. It seemed to be pulled up on each side much like the curtains in the old time movie theatres that are depicted in cartoons. Behind it was a sky of the most magnificent blue I had ever seen. It was blue, but it was also lavender, and again, it might have even had a golden cast to it. It was so bright that I thought it might hurt my eyes, but it did not. This sky was much like what I had seen when the sun set on the road to the village; very colorful and filled with hues not of this world. I stared at it for what seemed like a long time, but I knew that it really was not. Nothing was as it appeared. Time did not exist as I knew it. Everything was magnified; the sky, the grass, the flowers, everything. I do not remember seeing water, such as a stream, but I did see a path.

I felt I could not take it all in and yet I did. I knew that I was seeing something I had never experienced in my life before. I saw people. They were ordinary people, but beautiful in a different way from how we would describe them on earth. The sheer magnificence of the day radiated in their expressions of joy. They seemed to be wearing soft flowing robes made of a fabric I could not describe. It flowed softly about them like silk as they walked. I knew that I had never seen anything to compare with it in my world. The garments were in colors of blue but perhaps were they were a combination of blue and violet. They were pink, or could it have been peach? It might have been green or perhaps it might have been gold. I could not define a single color. They were so luminous and looked nothing like anything I had ever seen on earth. I was perplexed. I knew I had never seen colors like these before except in the Medjugorje sunset. They were brilliant, so brilliant that I expected that my eyes could not continue to look at them and yet, I never looked away. I took it all in. I was afloat in joy.

The people looked so happy and they were smiling. They almost drifted along. The people talked. I heard them and I think I understood them at the time even though I couldn't hear them with my ears. I had no idea what language they spoke. I felt so comfortable, so relaxed with them, but I knew somehow that I was not a part of the scene. I was just a spectator, nothing else.

As soon as the vision left me I could not remember a word of what had been said. I just remembered that they spoke and that there was laughter in their conversation. They carried books. Were they both men and women? Yes, I think so but I cannot be sure. They all looked so loving and kind. They appeared to be young adults, possibly in their late twenties or early thirties. I felt so delighted to be near them. And then, just as suddenly as it had come, the vision was gone. I could no longer see or hear them. There were no more vivid colors to be seen. The sky was back to the way it had been before the vision. I could not see bright green grass or brilliant flowers or people in gently flowing robes of many colors that glimmered. It all happened for me in a split second and yet, was it a split second? I could not tell. All concept of time had ceased to exist for me.

I was back in the field again and now it was just an ordinary earthly field. Suddenly my surroundings were muted and yet the sun was shining. I was again treading carefully so I would not to trip over a rock or step into a rut. I started to ask the others about what we had seen when I realized that the people ahead of me looked at me strangely and had no idea what I was talking about. I fell silent. For those who know me, that is impossible. I went back to the house with the group, had lunch, went over to the center of Medjugorje and carried on as though seeing what I had seen was nothing extraordinary given where I was. What could possibly happen after an experience such as this? With whom could I ever share this moment in time? I was not sure I could ever tell anyone about it. Once more I was alone in my thoughts.

My story stayed locked inside of me for months to come until I finally shared it with only one person, my husband. Who else would believe me? Years later, in October of 2011, Nate and I stood near the gravesite of Father Slavko, when I heard an account which finally explained in vivid detail what I had seen that day in the field returning from the castle. I knew then that once more I had witnessed a miracle and that the Holy Mother really does reveal things to us as she walks beside us on the roads and through the fields of Medjugorje.

We were standing just behind the grave of Father Slavko Barbaric. Franjo, our guide, was telling us stories of his youth with the visionaries in Medjugorje. He was also a young person at the time of the initial apparitions and Franjo was one of those who drove the children from place to place and helped to protect them from the police. I happened to mention to Franjo that I loved hearing stories of Jacov and shared one that had been told to me by Mirjana. Franjo laughed and told a story of his own about Jacov.

It seemed that the little boy was being a bit naughty one day. A nun standing nearby chided him by saying that she could not understand why the Holy Mother had chosen him and that he would not get to heaven with his behavior such as it was. Little Jacov piped up that the Holy Mother had taken him, showed him heaven and that there were no people there dressed in black and white as was the nun with whom he was speaking. He told her that the people there had worn soft gowns of a very silky material, not of this earth. He described the colors exactly as I had seen them. He said that some of the colors were pink, but perhaps peach, or lavender or maybe even gold. I knew then that I had seen what this little visionary had described. I cried inside my heart with love and joy thanking the Holy Spirit once again for another miracle. Yes, the first trip to Medjugorje certainly had been full of miracles. And, I knew that there would always be more to come.

One morning of that first trip, we hiked up Mt. Krisevac. It was cold and dark when we left Yelka's, but the first rays of the sun had started to appear as we arrived at the base of the mountain. Suddenly, it burst forth and bathed the surrounding countryside in the purest of gold light. The Stations of the Cross wind up the mountain so we stopped and prayed at each with Father White leading.

The rocks on the mountain are daunting. Most are white marble boulders, some of which have been polished to a shine in spots. Some of them were extremely large as well as slippery. The years of feet rubbing them and hands grasping and polishing them had caused treacherous conditions. We used walking sticks to steady our climb and our descent. One slip on loose rocks can be dangerous and it is important to be careful not to wedge a foot between the larger ones. I was aware of every challenge and prayed to the Holy Spirit to guide me and lead me to the top; to the cross at the summit. In spite of the challenges facing the pilgrims on the mountain, the thought of the magnificent white cross awaiting them drives them on with joy and anticipation. The first time you arrive at the summit is an incredible experience. The white forty foot cross built by the villagers back in the thirties in thanksgiving to Our Lord for his blessings, opens its arms in welcome. It beckons us to climb those last few harrowing feet to fall on our knees at its base and give honor and glory to God for his goodness and love. I took a photo of the cross that day which is depicted on the cover of this book.

I was so moved by what I saw spread out before me that I decided that this was the perfect place to make my first Medjugorje confession. Normally, a pilgrim would go to one of the thirty or forty priests stationed around the plaza of St. James Church. Never mind that I could visit any number of priests down there any day of the week, Oh no, I had to confess right up there on the mountain. I ran to Father White and asked if he would do me the honor of giving me absolution right out there at the top of the mountain in the bright noon day sun. He kindly agreed to my request and up we climbed further up, as high as we could go. There I knelt before heaven and asked for God's forgiveness and grace. The wind was fierce and strong. As I left, I realized that many people had seen us and that they had also decided that they wanted to confess in that glorious place. When I looked back, I saw a long line of people waiting to kneel before our kind and loving priest as he patiently sat, listened, blessed and absolved pilgrims by the dozens.

We arrived back at Yelka's somewhere around three. Father White was nowhere to be seen. About five thirty the poor man arrived, worn, tired and hungry, but with his wonderful smile intact. When I asked where he had been all that time, he simply looked at me. I could almost hear the Child Jesus asking His parents. "Did you not know that I was about my Father's business?" Amen.

Rita and Nate with Patrick, Nancy and fellow pilgrims at the Castle

Nate and Father Starbuck in Yelka's front yard

Our 2011 Pilgrim Group

St. James Church in Medjugorje Courtesy of Don Rowe

Marianne and Don Rowe's room at Ytlka's HouseCourttsy of Don Rowe

Pilgrims at the Blue Cross below Apparition Hill Courtesy of Don Rowe

Outside altar behind St. James Church during International Mass

The Rism Christ

Marianne Rowe walking on path toward St. James Church

Downtown area of Village of Medjugorje Courtesy of Don Rowe

"Dear Children,

Give thanks with me to the Most High for my presence with you. My heart is joyful watching the love and joy in the living of my messages. Many of you have responded but I wait for and seek all the hearts that have fallen asleep to awaken from the sleep of unbelief. Little children, draw even closer to my Immaculate Heart so that I can lead you all toward eternity. Thank you for having responded to my call."

Message: June 25, 2011

13

VEILS IN THE WIND

A PILGRIM SHOULD NEVER go to Medjugorje with the thought in mind that he or she will be granted miracles. Let go and let God is the best attitude to carry within ourselves. My first year in Medjugorje was filled with wonderful gifts from God and I never knew what was in store in the next hour or days or even years to come. Our hearts must be open if we are to see and feel the presence or Our Lady and her Son, Jesus. Not everyone will experience the same things. Let me give you a very good example.

Every afternoon at three o'clock, whoever was staying at Yelka's house would go out to the front garden where there was a beautiful gazebo. We gathered there with Father White, who would lead us in praying the Divine Mercy Chaplet. On this particular day the sky was bright and clear. From the gazebo we could see all the way to the top of Apparition Hill about a mile from where we sat. Several of us had our backs to the hill as we sat and prayed. I slowly became aware that a few people seated across from me were gazing at the top of the hill toward the brilliant white statue of our Holy Mother. People place prayer requests at the feet of the statue and the ground around it is covered with flowers left by the visiting pilgrims. I am always surprised to see that they all seem to be fresh each day.

As I turned around and looked behind me, I saw what appeared to be a woman, clothed all in white, a short distance away and higher on the hill from where the statue stood. I watched as the form became clearly defined. Veils began to blow in the wind and the figure came alive for me. At first, I doubted that what I was seeing was true. This happened following my experience of coming through the field from the castle and I started to seriously question my mind. Was I so enthralled with my concept of Medjugorje that my mind was playing tricks on me? Was I trying so hard in Medjugorje to take stories home in my heart that I was manufacturing them in my head? I sat there staring at the image on the hill and I heard others around me murmuring that they also could see the Virgin Mary up on the hill with her veils blowing in the wind. I was seeing what they were but I had certainly not verbalized the experience with anyone sitting around me. It was far too sacred.

Within moments, at least half of the people on my side of the gazebo had turned around and were gazing at the top of the hill as they recited the Chaplet. We all continued to pray. Those of us who could see the Our Mother continued to look in that direction. Others went on praying and appeared to be unaware that someone from heaven was with us. When we finished, some of our companions continued to pray or to chat and some stayed to stare quietly. I now had one more thing to share with my husband when I was ready to do so. Why some individuals saw and some did not I have never questioned. Each of us has private moments that we take away from this heaven on earth when we return home.

So much of what a person feels in Medjugorje stems from deeply spiritual private moments. In order to have such moments, a person has to be open to them. People need to see Medjugorje as it is, a place where one can become a child in Christ. We come to heal our souls. I had one such experience at the home of Ivan during my stay there. One would think that seeing some the things I did would make a person feel high strung, however, in my case, a warming sense of peace settled over me and I found myself very relaxed. I also realized that sleep eluded me and I was fine with that because all I wanted to do was to spend quiet moments in the chapel in Ivan's home. The rooms for the pilgrims are situated on the opposite side of the house from where the family resides. Those of us staying in the house had a separate entrance to the right of the main porch. When we entered the house, there was a tiny chapel on the left of the stairs leading to the pilgrim's rooms on the second floor. I always stopped on my way in or out of the house to kneel and say a little prayer in the peace and serenity of this candlelit room with the beautiful statue of The Holy Mother of Peace. I was comfortable there and I felt I could often be alone in the night with my prayers in that room if I was unable to sleep.

Eventually, I found myself in the chapel frequently and one night at about two o'clock I had read as much as I could so I decided to go down to the chapel to meditate. I knelt down but instead of meditating I suddenly started to pour out the story of my life and I experienced what I have heard described by many at the time of death when something akin to a video of our lives begins to unfold before us. My whole history from birth up to that moment in time seemed to explode before me and I remembered so much about not only my life, but the lives of my parents and my entire family. I was in the warm, candle lit room for a long time and I wept my heart out as I relived my life history. I didn't seem to have much control over what flashed before me. I remembered those who had been a part of me, many of whom I had lost in life through death.

The statue of Our Lady of Peace seemed to come alive as I poured out my sorrow at ever having hurt those whom I loved or should have loved. My body shook violently with sobs. When my experience was over, I felt vibrant and cleansed. It was as though the Holy Mother had been holding me in her arms and listening as only a mother can listen to her child. I don't think that I will ever be able to describe accurately to anyone the elation and joy I felt as I left the chapel that night. I do know that I slept in comfort and peace until the sun awakened me to another new day in Medjugorje. That morning the air was warm and bright and we all went to hear Jacov speak to us from the porch of his house next door.

While I am on the subject of chapels, I would like to mention also the beautiful one that Ivan had built separately on the property off to the side of his house. Nevis was given a key and had been invited to take us inside of the chapel because some of us were staying in Ivan's home. The chapel is private and for the use of the family from what I understand. The peace inside virtually wraps itself around you and its simplistic beauty is breathtaking. Medjugorje will always be heaven on earth to me. I am often asked why I want to travel to that far off place every year. Why not Lourdes or Fatima? I can only say that I feel a pull there. It is much like having your mother call to ask you to spend the summer with her. How can you not visit your mother when she calls so often, which Our Holy Mother does. I never have any doubt that she is there waiting to greet me.

"Dear Children!

These days I call you especially to open your hearts to the Holy Spirit. Especially during these days the Holy Spirit is working through you. Open your hearts and surrender your life to Jesus so that he works through your hearts and strengthens you in faith. Thank you for responding to my call."

Message: May 23, 1985

14

ANGELS

AFTER WE HAD BEEN in Medjugorje for awhile, Nina and I decided to venture out on our own. We shopped and we had lunch here and there and went looking for books about Medjugorje. One evening, Nina and I decided that we would climb to the top of Apparition Hill, where it all started, to say some prayers and return before the sun set. We invited Mary to come with us, but she was somewhat reluctant to go because the rocks can be so treacherous and it was getting late in the day. On the hill there are places where the gravel is loose and in other places there are large gaps between rocks where you must stretch your legs to cross. As on Cross Mountain, it is easy to wedge your foot between large rocks as you try to follow the path.

Mary expressed concern about our timing. It was after dinner and close to six o'clock so we had only an hour or so of good light in order to make the round trip up to the top and back down. Mary had been to Medjugorje several times. Since this was our first time. I want to say that we should have listened to the voice of wisdom and I would be right, but our persistence won out in the end and we prevailed upon Mary to come along. As we climbed, we separated at times, each choosing the easiest route for ourselves and praying privately as we ascended. We all reached the statue of our Holy Mother that looks out over the valley at about the same time and knelt together to pray. To the surprise of each of us, shadows began to lay quickly around us as the sun dipped very rapidly behind the surrounding hills.

We were warned of the impending darkness by Mary. Not one of us had thought to carry a flashlight. Why would we, the autumn sun was bright when we set out, but now here we were with the stars starting to appear in the darker areas of the sky above us. To say that we scurried as best we could to get down the treacherous path, as it became more and more difficult to follow is to say that it was easy to do. One does not scurry on a rocky hill. That was not the case. Suddenly, the sun left us and we were only halfway down the hill. The three of us were alone with very little light to guide us. Mary had slipped and fallen and the words of encouragement that Nina and I tried to muster had a very weak sound of confidence about them. Mary was not injured, but she had been right and I should have listened to her.

From out of nowhere, it appeared that we had company. A young man, perhaps in his early twenties, appeared beside us with a flashlight. He was going up the hill properly prepared and we were going down straining to see. He read our minds and changed his course to accompany us down to the bottom of the hill where safety awaited us. Just as he had appeared, he left us. I am not going to say that he was an angel even though I am sure he was. I have to admit that I just vaguely remember this part of our descent. I know that we were worried and a bit frightened at one moment and then relieved and grateful the next. I will leave it to you to decide what happened. It is said that if you ever get lost or need assistance in Medjugorje, there is always help to be found.

There is another thing that I will always remember about that evening on the Hill. During one of the times we climbed separately I looked down and saw a beautiful delicate flower at my feet. It was growing in the rocks in the most desolate and dry place imaginable. I knelt and bent way down with my nose almost touching the flower before I realized that it was an African Violet. They can be difficult to grow under the best of conditions. But, here it was, growing on a windy rocky hill with no tender loving care and with little or no water, where the temperature became cold and hostile as the night closed in upon its delicate petals.

Where had it come from, who had planted it there? Its survival was hard to imagine. It was much like the soul of man fighting against so many insurmountable odds, and yet it was worse for the tender little violet. It had not been given a free will and had little or no control over life. Finally, after much thought, I came to the conclusion that God planted it there and it is safe to say that the angels tended to it.

This brings me to another adventure that Nina and I shared. The day we went up to Cross Mountain and on the way down encountered the parade of Italian pilgrims behind us, we arrived at the bottom only to find that we could not see even one person in our group anywhere. There were no taxis available so we decided that the only way we could make our way back to Yelka's house was to hike. Of course, neither of us had any knowledge of which way to go. With a prayer to guide us, we set off to the right and promptly came to the inevitable fork in the road. We took the right fork and walked the distance of approximately two city blocks in the states and then decided that we were wrong. We turned and went back to where we started at the fork in the road. This time we went left. Again, we walked a short distance down a steep hill on a road that seemed to be going nowhere.

The two of us were starting to become a little nervous, so we once again turned around and returned to the corner we were growing to know so well. We tried to ask directions of some people we encountered, but they could not understand us and we could not understand them. We smiled, waved goodbye and stood still, trying to get our bearings. As we did, a little old car came rattling around the corner. It stopped in front of us and two young people, a man and a woman, jumped out and in perfect English asked where we were headed. Neither was native to Medjugorje and each had just arrived that morning.

By now, the sun was high and the day was hot. We were exhausted after climbing the mountain for several hours earlier. So without any hesitation, we climbed into the car, thanked the young people and trusted that our guardian angels would get us back to the village safe and sound. In no time we spotted a landmark that we knew and before long we found ourselves a short distance from Yelka's house. We arrived just about in time for dinner. I never doubted again that somebody would rescue me if I got lost in Medjugorje. Angels are everywhere in Medjugorje, but then our Guardian Angels are always with us everywhere and at all times. After all, they do have jobs.

"Dear Children,

As the Queen of Peace, I desire to give peace to you, my children, true peace which comes through the heart of my Divine Son. As a mother, I pray that wisdom, humility and goodness may come to reign in your hearts, that peace may reign, that my Son may reign. When my son will be ruler you will be able to help others to come to know him.

When heavenly peace comes to rule over you, those who are seeking it in the wrong places, thus causing pain to my heavenly heart, will recognize it .My children, great will be my joy when I see that you are accepting my words and that you desire to follow me. Do not be afraid, you are not alone. Give me your hands and I will lead you. Do not forget your Shepherds. Pray that in their thoughts they may always be with my son who called them to witness Him. Thank you for responding to my call."

Message: April 2, 2012

15

AVE MARIA

AS I WEAVE MY way through the moments and memories of my first days in Medjugorje, I am reminded of the people I met or encountered there. One who comes to mind is the man I mentioned earlier when I described the amazing voice of the gentleman in the choir. It did not take me long to learn his identity. Actually, he turned out to be very well known in Medjugorje, dear to everyone in the village, and to every pilgrim who ever visited this piece of heaven on earth.

Each morning, as we came into breakfast the first thing many of us did was check the events of the day which were listed on a board in the kitchen. Nevis would plan activities, including such things as going to hear an apparitionist speak or visiting a special place. One of those places, The Mothers Village comes to mind. The village had been developed to help mothers raise their young after the war that had torn their lives apart. Incidentally, the priest, Father Svetozar Kraljevic, Founder and current Director of the Mother's Village, reminded me of my father, who died in August of 1980. I found myself looking for him in Medjugorje because he looked so much like my father. I miss my dad very much and it occurred to me that this might be another gift. There are all kinds of miracles in Medjugorje.

There is always so much to see, to hear and to experience and Nevis was helping us to do everything. On one particular day the board indicated that we were to attend a concert given in the yellow building behind the village church of St. James. It was to be performed by a singer named David Parkes. As David walked on stage, I immediately recognized him as the singer with whom I had harmonized in the choir. David was the man with the voice of the Angel Gabriel, the man who's rendering of the Ave Maria still lingered in my mind. I was stricken with a major dose of humility. I harmonized with him! Tears flowed down my checks when, at the beginning of the concert, the hymn flowed from his lips effortlessly from deep inside him. His voice was as resonant with the music as it would have been had God had planted it deep inside Davie long before he was born to this earth. Of course, God did. David sang as naturally as we speak. The concert hall fell silent all through the music and for many minutes after the last note floated back up to heaven from where it had come.

David is a man of many talents. Born in Ireland of loving and devout parents he began singing in church as a child. Then his early teenage years saw him grow into a strong soccer player. He went on to become an international star playing with the likes of Pele. Success took its toll on David and he grew away from the God of his childhood to the god of his fame. He became bigger than life as his soccer career blossomed and eventually led him to even more glamorous exploits on the stage, this time as an international singing star playing in countries all throughout the world.

As fame and fortune grew greater for David, his wife and family grew less important and he eventually turned away from the goodness of his past. David was in his early thirties when he was diagnosed with Crones disease and had a death sentence hovering over him. At this point, with total separation from God and family, a miracle brought David to Medjugorje and back to God kicking and screaming. That is when the unimaginable happened; David, who no longer believed in God at that moment in time, was slain in the Spirit and was instantly cured of the disease.

Today he is giving back. David is sharing the gifts of God's love, his voice and his testimony of healing with those who are blessed to hear him each week during the time of the year that he works in Medjugorje. It costs nothing to spend the evening with David to bask in the warmth of his personality and his magnificent voice. The first time I heard David in concert, he began with his testimony of conversion, with the story of his life, his stories of triumph and suffering, his pride and his miseries, his losses and his moments of glory with his Savior. My husband and I, as the years went on, made it a point to approach David after his concerts to thank him for being there for us. We were personally blessed to visit with him in the US in the small town of Mesquite, NV. David remembered my husband from Medjugorje but had no idea who I was.

Humility is good for the soul and it seems that each encounter I have with David makes me more and more aware of my need to have another cup of it. While in Medjugorje, anyone can hear him sing, listen to stories of the miracles of his life and near death experience and his return to the grace of God. David sings a song of love and humility. It is based on the song "My Way" made famous by Frank Sinatra. David puts a different spin on his rendition and has changed the name to "I did it God's Way!" We should all adopt this as our song of life and do everything Gods way.

If you go to Medjugorje and you see David, please tell him we both said hello! He will probably remember my husband, Nate. By the way, I always pop in my CD and I listen to David sing in my car. Guess what I listen to the most. You have two choices now. Thank you, David. We are always happy to see and hear you. May the road rise up to meet you and the wind be always at your back and may God bless you at every moment of your life.

Dear Children,

Also today with joy, I desire to give you my motherly blessing and to call you to prayer. May prayer become a need for you to grow more in holiness every day. Work more on your, conversion because you are far away, little children. Thank you for having responded to my call."

Message: March 25, 2012

16

REMEMBER...

U P UNTIL NOW, I have shared stories of things that happened on the first trip that I took to Medjugorje. But there are many experiences from later trips to share as well. When I think of the first time that my husband came with me to my home away from home, I am reminded again of my dear friend Michelle's words, "Remember it is a pilgrimage not a vacation". If you ever plan to visit Medjugorje, I ask you please to never forget that phrase.

Nate and I set out for Las Vegas very well prepared for our trip to Chicago, where we were to meet up with our tour group. We left our home in St. George, Utah with plenty of time to catch our flight. Everything went well at check-in. We had not stayed overnight anywhere in the city and we got to the airport in plenty of time to board our flight which was scheduled to arrive into Chicago several hours before take-off to Vienna. As I recall, I had planned for a six hour layover hoping it would give us plenty of time to connect to our next flight. I made sure that I ate at the airport while we were waiting. I did not want to make the same mistake twice. I had to plan carefully since Chicago was two hours ahead of Las Vegas. I ended up having to eat again. Better safe than sorry.

Wow, did we ever have plenty of time! It turned out that we had about five hours to sit and wait. Our flight was delayed because the plane was still back in Los Angeles because of "weather". I am not sure where the "weather" was. The weather service reported that it was bright and sunny that day in LA. Then the flight was reported delayed again, this time because of mechanical difficulties. I don't think it was our plane that had mechanical difficulties, but nobody actually said that. They never do. When a plane finally arrived to take us to Chicago, there was no room on the flight that came to pick us up because by now more people had arrived and were waiting. The boarding area was mobbed. Two plane loads of passengers were waiting to board. All kinds of people were giving up their seats in order to be awarded free flights at a later time. We were five hours behind schedule when we took off, but the cabin crew assured us that we would be in on time to catch our connecting flight. Isn't that interesting? Oh, but not to worry!

We were in a landing pattern to the Chicago area when a storm rolled in. Our pilot ascended and circled around until it was safe to put down. Of course, a whole lot of other pilots did the same, so we all lined up one by one and each plane landed safely only to sit out on the runway for what seemed like an eternity waiting for a gate to clear. At this point, we had about fifty minutes to deplane and make our way to our flight going to Vienna. As it turned out, the flight to Vienna was delayed also, so if we had played out cards right, we might have made it to the gate on time. However, as luck would have it, as the old saying goes, the crew decided to help us and suggested that they have wheel chairs waiting for us right inside the terminal. The wheel chair "drivers" would then whisk us off from Terminal 1 where we landed and over to Terminal 5 to the International Departure gate. If you have ever been to O'Hare Airport, you know that Terminal 5 is probably three miles away from Terminal 1 at best.

Nate and I became hysterical laughing at the thought that two perfectly healthy people were being pushed at a snail's pace through this ridiculously complex airport. We were on moving walkways and escalators. We actually had to get up and out of the wheel chairs to walk down on the escalators on our own. People laughed. We had to be pushed out into the street at one point to get to the International Terminal. This time I was laughing even harder. Cars were whizzing by us and we had people honking at us to get out of the way. I had a great big man pushing me and Nate had a small woman. Go figure. Actually, we could have walked or run faster on our own pulling an elephant behind us, but since we are polite people or simple minded, as the case may be, we bought into this insane plan.

We arrived at our gate one minute after the door to the aircraft closed, and, of course, were forbidden to board. The ground crew member at the desk told us that if we went to the window, we could look out, watch our plane pull away and wave to our friends. So, we went to the window, waved goodbye and blew kisses to them. Our wheelchair drivers hung their heads and apologized. They also offered to take us to wherever we had to go next. My husband gave them each a tip.

When you are going on a religious pilgrimage, it does not seem appropriate to throw a fit, so we didn't. We simply walked to the podium and asked for our options. We were told that another flight was going out in about forty five minutes, but we would have to go back to Terminal 1 and change our tickets to get on board. We were told to run. Since our kind friends with the wheel chairs were still nearby, they offered to push us back. We did get there with a little time to spare, but then were told that since we were part of a large group of pilgrims, they would have to research our reservations for cost and at the moment they could not find any evidence that we ever had any. That makes perfect sense. Uh huh.

We stood at the desk in Terminal 1 as time ticked on. The person who was helping us had to leave to go out to dinner and a new person took over our cause. Of course, that meant explaining everything all over again when she finally arrived. She printed new tickets, but by now the second flight had left and there we stood holding reservations again for a flight that was now was in the air. Somebody suggested that we might try to fly out on Lufthansa to Dubrovnik by way of Frankfurt, Germany, so back we went back to another gate in Terminal 5. Our wheel chair drivers had nothing else to do, so they ran us all the way. Actually, there was no need to run, because the Lufthansa flight was not due to leave until ten that evening. It was now six thirty. This meant that by the time we made it to Frankfurt, our flight to Dubrovnik would get us in after our fellow pilgrims had been picked up by the bus driver for the ride to Medjugorje. If none of this makes sense, don't try to read it again. It does not make sense to me and I am writing it.

After obtaining reservations on Lufthansa, we sat in the boarding area for hours waiting for our flight to load. The plane arrived late. We did have time to eat and while we waited our entertainment was provided by a man who owned a blueberry farm in Maine. He was on his way to sell his blueberries to somebody in Europe and he was on his cell phone speaking with a person who was trying to tell him in broken English that they didn't want the blueberries anymore. Many other people getting on the flight with us spoke no English and we spoke no German so when the blueberry man gave up and went home, we sat and read old discarded newspapers.

We were warned by the ticket agent that we might not have any luggage when we got to Europe because it probably was put on the second flight we missed in Chicago. It could be on its way to Vienna. Who knew? We eventually made it on board and sat down to relax knowing that we were finally on our way. Now, I had another surprise in store .At that time in my life I had a severe neck problem and I was in a great deal of pain. I had brought along a special pillow to get my spine up and off the seat of the aircraft and I was armed with pain killers. The only thing that I did not have was a baseball bat, which I could have used during the flight to help the five year old behind me get some sleep. His mother was wearing a burka and I was not inclined to be in the least bit rude to her or her child. It is not politically correct to do that. I did complain, but just a little. The child kicked the back to my seat for the entire duration of the trip. He talked, he cried and he ran up and down the aisle for hours! No amount of dirty looks, calling for the flight attendant to intercede or glaring at the mother had any affect. The mother looked very apologetic. The child kicked and misbehaved and my neck screamed in pain all night long.

We arrived in Frankfurt only to find that we could not read the directional signs in the airport. When we finally found our departure lounge, we were told to go back to the arrival area and pick up our bags. It seemed that somebody had violated security and all bags had to be sent through the scanners again before we could board the aircraft. We had to go out of the secured area to retrieve our checked luggage. Of course, our luggage was not there, so we simply went through the process with only our carry-on bags. We then had to explain that we had no idea where our checked-in items had been sent. That was interesting. After trying to explain the situation to a German speaking airline representative, we were turned over to someone who spoke English. He was from Boston. Except for the fact that his words that started with an "a" sounded like an "r" and his "r" words sounded like "a" words, we both understood him perfectly, especially Nate who also hails from Massachusetts. Eventually, we were able to board the next flight in our journey.

In Dubrovnik, I was excited to see my big red suitcase sitting on the carousel waiting to be retrieved. It had arrived with our friends on the first flight. Apparently, our luggage made it to the flight as we were being wheeled around the airport in Chicago. Our friends had not seen us waving goodbye and they wondered why our bags were there and we weren't. Next time I am going to climb into my bag and go with it. I was delighted when Nate's luggage showed up on the other side of the same carousel as mine.

The next big surprise was seeing Frank, the husband of Nevis, standing near the exit door waiting for us. The bus to Medjugorje had left about an hour before taking all of our fellow pilgrims up into the countryside. Frank had arranged for a taxi to take us to the home of Yelka, where we were welcomed with open and loving arms. I certainly was learning how to make a grand entrance. I was sure that nobody would ever volunteer to travel with me. The taxi cost $85.US, but it was worth every penny even though the driver was not exactly sure how to get to Medjugorje. After a few unusual turns, we arrived at our destination. Eventually we were reimbursed by the insurance we had purchased for the trip. However, I had to fight for months to get the additional cost of the flight on Lufthansa. I did not get a group or tourist rate. In Michelle's words, if you go, remember it is a pilgrimage, not a vacation.

"Dear Children,

Also today I call you to prayer. Little children, prayer works miracles. When you are tired and sick and you do not know the meaning of your life, take the rosary and pray. Pray until the prayer becomes for you a joyful meeting with your savior. I am with you little children and I intercede and pray for you. Thank you for having responded to my call."

Message: April 25, 2001

17

JUST FOR NATE

THE MIRACLES OF MEDJUGORJE were not limited to the time I traveled on my own. On one of the trips that Nate and I took together, I was saddened by the fact that he had not experienced any of the wonders that I had while I was there by myself. It was the last day of our pilgrimage. Even though he said that he was not there for miracles; that he felt peace and love in his heart, I felt badly that he had not experienced some of the things that I had. It was a Friday and our last day. We strolled over to the plaza to go to confession, but we were early. It might have been around five fifteen as we sat down in the large amphitheater behind the church. We had a half hour to go before confessions started and we sat there looking up into the sky discussing our thoughts about Medjugorje and what beautiful weather we had enjoyed.

On this trip we were able to see so much together. We had visited the waterfalls, which I had never seen and Nate had gotten to know Rikki, the dog of Yelka and her husband. He fell in love with the big yellow dog with the short legs, who slept upside down under a table on the patio. Nate also got to know Father White and spent quite a lot of time with him. We all walked through the fields together and had visited Cenacolo, where we heard testimonies from the young addicted men whose lives were beginning to heal. We were together when we saw Mirjana during her apparition there on October 2nd. Nate and Frank grew to know each other well and enjoyed long conversations together after dinner in the evenings. I believe this was also the trip when Nate had his first taste of white lightening from the still of Marco, the father of Yelka. I think that Nate had a very nice time getting to know everything and everybody.

This was when we spent a lot of time with Laurie, who was accompanied by her young daughter Mary Beth. We did so much together, including going off to Dubrovnik one day. We visited churches and museums and attended mass at the Church of St. Blaise, the Patron Saint of the City of Dubrovnik. In the evening, we would all go out to the local pub and have pizza. This is probably the only pub in the world where a signed photograph of Pope John Paul ll hangs in an honored spot above the door. If I knew the story of why it is there, I would share it with you. I do know that it was given personally to the owners, who have become our friends over the years. All was wonderful in Medjugorje even before the blessed event, the miracle, which I am about to describe to you, a miracle just for Nate.

I have mentioned that Our Holy Mother appears in this heavenly place every day at five forty. That evening as Nate and I sat staring up at the sky, which was cloudless, we could see both Apparition Hill in front of us and Cross Mountain in the distance. The sky was a beautiful blue and the sun was beginning to set in the west. As we gazed upward, a large cloud column began to form. At the top of the column, we started to see what looked like a head beginning to appear and then the column taking the shape of a woman. The next thing we saw was the entire figure of a woman holding an infant in her left arm. She was looking down at the child. Veils appeared on each side of the mother and her child and they blew gently in the breeze. Our Lady was standing on a cloud. I could not look away and I quietly asked Nate if he could see what I was seeing. He said yes. For me, the face of the woman came into focus and I could see the eyes and the mouth perfectly formed. Nate has said that he does not remember seeing those features. We gazed at this vision for what seemed like ten minutes and again, as I had experienced when I had seen heaven on earth, everything disappeared as quickly as it had come. The clouds did not just melt away, they simply vanished and the sky was all blue again. As I sit and remember those moments, I will always wonder why we were chosen to be so blessed.

At five forty, just a minute or two later, we saw a brilliant ball of white light shoot across the sky toward Cross Mountain. From there we saw a line of clouds, that looked like dashes, form an arc over to Apparition Hill to where the statue of Our Mother stood. The line stopped above the statue and a shaft of light shown straight down upon it. At the end of the daily apparition time, the shaft of light instantly disappeared. Nate and I looked around to see if anyone seated near us had seen what we had witnessed but it did not appear to us that anyone had. Nobody else was looking up to the sky or over toward the hill. We quietly got up, went over to the plaza, looked for an English speaking priest and went to confession. After that, we went for the International Evening mass. When it ended we stayed for Adoration of the Blessed Sacrament. At nine o'clock we left and walked back through the fields under the stars toward Yelka's house.

I would like to mention here that what we experienced in the sky behind the Church of St. James took place in 2007. Once again, it was difficult for me to tell anyone what I had seen, but this time my husband had witnessed the vision too. When Wayne Weible came to St. George, Nate gave a talk at the Holiday Inn, and he spoke of this experience with much emotion. Four years later, in 2011, I purchased a book by a man named Thomas Rutkowski, a very blessed man from Pennsylvania, who had been to Medjugorje. On the cover of the book called, "The Apostles of the Last Days", was a photograph that had been taken on his farm. It was not absolutely identical to what we had seen, but it was a very clear cloud formation showing the figure of Our Holy Mother holding the Child Jesus in her arms.

Included in the cloud formation was a horizontal cloud, which in conjunction with the, figure formed a perfect cross. We did not see a cross as we looked up at the sky in 2007, and Our Mother was fully facing us. But Tom's photo was still very much like what we had seen; the Mother and the Child formed from clouds. The photo on the cover of the book assured us that we really did see what we thought we had. I just found this book a short time ago after I had written about the vision, and once again, I was grateful that my imagination was not playing tricks on me or on Nate, for that matter. Once again, I feel I had the help of either the Holy Spirit or an angel to help me feel confident that what we saw was real.

"Dear Children, Do you not know how many graces God is giving you?

You do not want to move ahead these days when the Holy Spirit is working in a special way. Your hearts are turned toward the things of earth and they preoccupy you. Turn your hearts toward prayer and seek the Holy Spirit to be poured out on you. Thank you for having responded to my call."

Message: May 9, 1985

18

SOLO, BUT NOT ALONE

I N 2008 WE HAD gone up to the mountains in Colorado for our usual escape from the heat at our home in St. George and I had great expectations of taking the trip to Medjugorje for the third time, this time with Nate and some dear friends. God had other plans for me. This time I was the one who was to stay home and let my husband have his time in Medjugorje. Each year after our visit, we would come back to St. George and tell our friends all about our trip and encourage our fellow parishioners to join us for the next.

This year, our friends, Ruth and Cliff joined Nate. They come from Idaho to St. George each year to spend the winter. They were with us when we had our yearly presentation and this particular year, they had the good fortune to hear Wayne Weible speak. I am sure you remember that I mentioned that Wayne wanted to come to St. George and that he was finally able to come for a book signing. After the presentation by Wayne, Ruth and Cliff decided to go on the pilgrimage and we were delighted.

Fortunately, that year, I purchased trip insurance and I even got to use it. I had been having severe pain in my upper back and decided to see my doctor. The prognosis, after a myriad of tests, indicated significant spinal damage in the area of the base of my skull. I needed surgery.

My spinal column would have to be fused. I tried to ignore the idea of an operation and decided that I would take care of the nuisance after my return from our trip in October. My doctor in Colorado had other plans, so I would not be joining Cliff ,Ruth and Nate in Medjugorje that year.

I had the operation in early September in Fort Collins, Colorado and by the end of the month, it was agreed that I could stay behind at our home in the mountains to recuperate with my dogs as company. Nate had to leave without me, but he was able to meet up with Cliff and Ruth to begin their pilgrimage by flying out of Dulles in Washington, DC. They went on to Vienna and then to Split where they joined the rest of their group. Once again the pilgrims stayed at the home of Yelka. Nevis was their guide.

I asked Cliff to tell me what the highlight of the trip was for him and he talked about the beauty of the place and all of their travels. When the sun came up in the conversation, Cliff, as many others before and after him did, told of how the sun had held their attention for a good twenty minutes. Cliff described the experience he and Ruth had of looking directly at the sun. First came the magnificent colors; once again, not of this world.

The colors were hard for them to describe except for the fact that they are so deep and so vivid. At one point, Cliff told me that the sun looked as if it was outlined with pink cotton candy. Next he described darts of light shooting out in all directions around the sun. After that amazing display, the sun began to leap and jump all over the sky. All of this happens at sunset and before you know it, the sun drops and darkness fills the world. Not everyone sees the miracles of the sun and the experiences are not all the same. We have a friend who has gone to Medjugorje at least twenty times and tells us that he has never seen any amazing sights or miracles. He also says he needs no proof of God's divinity or power. He has Parkinson's, but nothing slows him down. We think of him as another modern day saint. We love him and we are always happy to have him with us on our pilgrimages. When I remember what I have seen the sun do, I sometimes think that mankind has tried to duplicate the amazing antics of the sun. I know now that even fireworks fall short. Man is man and God is God and I know it will be that way until the end of time. After arriving home, Cliff asked the doctor if he had sustained any sun damage to his eyes for having stared at the sun. The doctor answered. "No Cliff, its old age."

On the trip with Cliff and Ruth, Nate had quite an experience one night. He and Cliff and Ruth had gone to see David Parkes' concert in the yellow building behind the church. Earlier that day Nate had met a couple from Ireland in the village and they had asked about things to do and see in Medjugorje. Nate volunteered that David Parke was appearing that evening in concert and gave them information and directions as to where to find the yellow building. That evening, after the conclusion of David's performance, Nate ran into the couple and started to carry on a conversation with them. In the interim, the group from Yelka's, including Ruth and Cliff, had gone on to make their way back to Yelka's house.

Taxis were becoming scarce by the time everyone from the concert got to the street and the last taxi rolled up, Nate had not yet found his way back to his companions. Ruth and Cliff had no idea that he was still back at the hall and they were persuaded to take the last taxi. They were very distressed at the thought of leaving Nate behind, but thought that perhaps he had gone on ahead without them. When he finally made his way to the taxi stand, the road outside the front of the church was deserted and Nate was left with one choice. That choice was to make his way home through the dark vineyards under a moonless and starless sky.

The walk thought the fields and vineyards without a flashlight is next to impossible. There are very large rocks on parts of the path. There are holes too. You can see them in the daylight, but at night they virtually disappear. The paths often take abrupt twists and turns and the ruts are deep, sometimes deep enough to break an ankle. Normally, one would meet up with somebody on the path, but that night there was nobody there. It took Nate double the time to make his way back to Yelka's as he tried to decipher the way to go. Near the end of the path, he managed to meet up with two young men who were carrying a flashlight. (You are never lost in Medjugorje.) Finally, after a very long time, Nate arrived at the turn to Yelka's house only to run into a very worried and frightened Cliff who had been pacing nervously at the disappearance of his friend.

This story had a happy ending, Nate was home safe and he tells me he prayed every step of the way.

"Dear Children,

I am with you for so much time and already for so long. I have been pointing you to God's presence and his infinite love which I desire for all of you to come to know. And, you, my children? You continue to be deaf and blind as you look at the world around you and do not want to see where it is going without my Son. You are renouncing Him and He is the source of all graces. You listen to me while I am speaking. But your hearts are closed and you are not hearing me. You are not praying to the Holy Spirit to illuminate you.

My children, pride has come to rule. I am pointing out humility to you. My children, remember that only a humble soul shines with purity and beauty because it has come to know the love of God. Only a humble soul becomes heaven because my Son is in it. Again, I implore you to pray for those my Son has chosen, those are your Shepherds. Thank you for responding to my call."

Message: February 2, 2012

19

THE QUIET VOICE

THE WALK THROUGH THE vineyards that I just described brings to my mind an adventure I had that was very similar to Nate's but a little more eventful. But before I tell that story, I have another one to describe. In 2010, we went off on our pilgrimage with two dear friends, Marianne and Don Rowe. This trip was not without moments of sheer panic. When we arrived at the Las Vegas airport we had a surprise waiting for us. After months of planning, our trip packages had arrived and every detail appeared to be absolutely perfect. We all had everything required to get off on time and meet up with our fellow travelers. At least we thought so.

When we arrived at the airport in the very early hours, we were all astounded to find out that Marianne was not booked on the flight. She was told that even though she was holding her hard tickets in her hand, that she had no reservations. Make sense? No, of course it did not. We were going to Medjugorje. It is a pilgrimage, remember? We all just stood staring at Marianne, who said she would go home and wait for us to get back. That was never going to happen.

Marianne was escorted off to the side with an airline official who called 206 Tours in New York. Fortunately, the office was open and everything was straightened out quickly. Unfortunately, though, Marianne and Don were separated on the first leg of the trip and were unable to sit together on the first flight. They did, however, have seats together during the next portion of the outbound flights and we all arrived at our destination together. Coming home, everything went smoothly. Praise God. Please remember the stories that I have shared with you if you travel to Medjugorje. Know that in the end, The Holy Spirit and Our Holy Mother will come to your rescue. What I found most interesting about this experience is that I had completely forgotten what had happened. So did Marianne and Don. Only Nate remembered and so I was able to tell you about it.

Believe it or not, there is more to share about the events of this trip. One afternoon around three, the four of us left Yelka's house to explore the village. Fortunately, Don bought a flashlight while we were in town. When it was time to make our way back to the house, we decided that we would have something to eat where we were and then go to the church for the International Mass.

It was a beautiful day. As planned we went to mass and devotions. We then headed to the taxi stand to return home. At that point in time I was ready to ride back. It had been a long day. However, Nate wanted to walk because it was such a pleasant night. This time the sky was filled with stars and the moon was bright and full. I did not see the walk as terribly pleasant in spite of the conditions. Something kept nagging at me to take the taxi, but I lost the vote and off we went through the fields. It was very dark when we set out.

A quiet voice kept telling me that we should take the taxi. I tried to convince my husband of that, but it was, after all, a beautiful night for walking and I gave in. Because we had left so early in the afternoon, I had not carried our flashlights in my bag. Fortunately, Don and Marianne now had two of them so they used one and loaned the other to us. I was carrying the light, and the beam was ahead of us, but for some reason, I handed it to Nate, who was behind me. When we got within a short distance of the house, Nate suggested that we cut through a neighbor's front yard. I was not in favor of doing so because on my first trip to Medjugorje I had found myself being scolded by that very same neighbor for cutting through her property and I knew not to go there. I tried to convince my husband not to take the short cut only to be told that it was dark and if we were quiet, nobody would know we were there. After a short discussion, I gave in again.

As we approached the house, the flashlight beam was no longer illuminating the path in front of me and seconds later I found myself falling headlong onto a cement sidewalk after tripping over the lip of the walkway where it stepped up off the path. I heard a very loud crack as I hit the cement and then felt the blood starting to spurt out of my forehead. The blood was everywhere and it was impossible to stem the flow. I sat there dazed, thinking again that I was about to die again in Medjugorje. (This was getting to be a very common occurrence.) I was amazed that the people in the house had not heard the commotion. Finally, it was decided that with help I could get up and walk to the house where all of our friends were gathered for an evening snack. When we arrived, I managed to get blood all over everything and, of course, I was immediately wrapped in hugs. Fortunately, we had four helpers who all turned out to be nurses, one of whom had worked in emergency for thirty years. God is good.

For the first time since I had been going to Medjugorje, as I recall, there was an emergency facility set up behind the church. It was being run by the Knights of Malta and the emergency room was staffed by German speaking doctors and nurses. I was rushed off by taxi to the facility in the company of my body guards, Nate, Marianne and Don. Before I knew it, I was on an examining table looking up at the biggest doctor I had ever seen in my life. He had to be at least six foot seven or more. When I asked if he planned to deaden my forehead before sewing it up, my question was met with a grunt so I just closed my mouth and quietly took each stitch as it came. I could hear Nate across the room groaning and cringing as each one was administered. It really was not all that bad and I had no intention to complain.

All during the night I sat straight up in my bed to sleep because I was told that if I had a concussion, I had to stay awake or I could die. I took this very seriously. My sister died at age 46 because of a similar accident. She fell down a flight of stairs, sustained a concussion and was dead on the living room sofa in the morning. This is not something one ever forgets.

During the longest night of my life, I would fall over occasionally, but never far enough to do serious further damage. As I sat there watching shadows on the wall, I pondered what the neighbors would think in the morning. Would they wonder if a wild animal had been shot in their front yard the night before? I had never seen a wild animal in Medjugorje, so I adjusted my question to suggest a cow instead. I left quite a mess to be cleaned up. If I had been back in St. George, I might have grabbed a bucket and offered to scrub the sidewalk the next day. I certainly did not want that woman to chew me out again. I should not have cut through her front yard. I knew that!

In the morning I thought that I looked pretty good considering the circumstances of the night before. My face showed little sign of bruising and aside from the enormous four by six inch bandage on the right side of my forehead; nobody would ever guess that anything had happened. The night before, the nurses I had warned me that I would look more like a purple water balloon than a person when I got up. I was feeling great. My face was pretty normal and I was still alive for the second time on a trip to Medjugorje. I gloated to the nurses that I was sure that my face would never swell. However, when I awakened to the second morning, my face was green, purple, black, orange, magenta and puce, I think. I say I think, because my right eye refused to open and remained that way for about three days. I couldn't see much. Nevis stopped me as I came down the stairs with "What happened to you?. Apparently she had not noticed any damage the day before either.

I wore dark glasses everywhere I went for the sake of others. As a matter of fact, I took off the glasses in the Frankfurt airport on the way home and some man took one look at me, let out a little yelp then turned and walked away quickly. We were in a restaurant and I don't think he finished his lunch. Strangely, by the time I arrived at my home in St. George, my coloring had returned to normal, but the lump on my temple stuck up about a quarter of an inch for several weeks. That was a year and a half ago and I still have a little reminder bump. All of this brings me to a point that I would like to state loud and clear; when the Holy Spirit speaks, listen to him. Take the taxi! That little voice in my head was none other than His. I should know, I hear it all the time.

While we are still on the subject of our trip with Marianne and Don, I would like to tell you a little more about the miracles of the sun. There is a wonderful area to visit in Medjugorje. Pilgrims go there to recite the Rosary, visit the Risen Christ statue, and to pay respect to those buried in the cemetery, where the body of Father Barbaric is interned. This area is behind the church. Marianne and Don were there one afternoon. As you walk along the paths in the early evening, you are looking at the western sky and you are in a perfect place to see the sun set.

One evening, as the sun dipped low on the western horizon, Marianne saw what appeared to be beautiful blue gemstones surrounding the sun. The gemstones appeared to be like crystal, sparkling and creating a round frame encircling the golden sun. When Marianne quietly told Don what she was seeing, he told her not to look at the sun for fear that she would damage her eyes. Nate and I were not made aware of what Marianne had seen that day.

The next afternoon, Nate and I had gone over to the plaza outside the church to go to confession. That day we were with Marianne and Don, but left them and went right over to an English speaking priest almost immediately after we arrived. Our confessions took a short time and in a few minutes we were able to rejoin the two of them. Don was walking quickly toward us and he was obviously very excited. Marianne had gone off for a few minutes and Don walked over beyond the church toward the west. The sun was very low and in the middle of it Don saw a perfect heart, which he described as the shape of a valentine heart. He called to Marianne and she saw the identical heart right in the middle of the bright white sun. Don wanted us to see the sun too, but it appeared that we were too late. We started to walk down the path toward the Risen Christ and suddenly there it was again. This time the sun started to pulsate before us. Then I saw the Sacred Host form and the Sacred Heart of Jesus begin to take shape in the middle of it. What I saw was not a valentine heart, but an actual beating heart in the middle of the sun. Next, I watched it come close to us and then pull away. Incredible colors would come and go as the sun danced and twirled before me. I saw the deepest blue I had ever seen surrounded by a very deep dark blood red color. Then the entire sun itself turned to the very dark blood red before it became outlined with brilliant gold. I stood transfixed, unable to move from the spot.

None of us knew if we were seeing was what any of the rest of us could see. We stood there for about fifteen minutes and then, to compare notes, we stood side by side looking at the sun. We told each other what we were experiencing; the colors, the actions, the signs. They were all the same. We opened our eyes and continued to watch. The miracle of the sun had come for us again, and yet, there were pilgrims walking by with no realization of what had happened in the sky before them. Some people looked at us, looked toward the direction in which we were staring and with absolutely no expression of wonder just turned and walked away. Others stopped and stared in awe as we did. Those who had moved on could not see because they were closed to the actions of God. Some people experience incredible signs, others do not. There is no explanation. This dancing, pulsating, sun in Medjugorje is the same as the one that appeared in Fatima before the beginning of the First World War. Our Holy Mother tells us that Medjugorje is the continuation of Fatima and the sun is there to prove it.

Don has asked me to share one more thing with you. Each evening when we went to the International Masses, we took little radios with us which we could turn to a frequency where we could find our own individual language. The mass was said in Croatian, German, Italian, Polish, English and others. I mentioned this earlier in the book, but repeat it so that if you go to Medjugorje, you will be sure to ask for or buy one of these radios. Our host family provided them. It would have been very difficult to sit through two hours of the mass not knowing what was being said, however, with our little translation radios, we were able to hear everything in our language making it easy for us to participate fully. Don felt that it must have been like the first Pentecost when the Holy Spirit enabled the apostles to speak and listen in the many languages of the people.

This was not our last trip to Medjugorje. Nate and I went again in 2011 and were joined by Mary, Bob, Inga, Ron and Sharon; all members of our church in St. George. We shared a beautiful afternoon together when we heard mass celebrated by Father Jim Starbuck at the Chapel of Diving Mercy on the other side of Apparition Hill, where we all know by now that Our Holy Mother first appeared. We thank them all so much for joining us on this journey. There were some minor mix ups on the trip coming and going, but at this point in time all I can say is, yes, I know, it is not a vacation. I warn everybody of this. It should never be a surprise. I was pretty used to it by the last trip and I have become ready for just about anything to happen in the future. Satan does not want us to go to visit our Holy Mother, so he makes every trip as frustrating as he can. We did many things on this trip just as we had during all the previous ones and all of us received graces.

On the last trip that we took to Medjugorje, we visited some new places that we had never been to before, such as the Garden of St. Francis outside of the Mother's Village. It is one of the most beautiful wooded areas I have ever seen in my life. We also made a close friend in Franjo, our guide, who took us from place to place to find new wonders and experience new things. The trip reunited us with old friends and acquainted us with new ones. Patrick and Nancy were still there, still loving and still kind. The Castle, Our Lady of the Sacred

Heart Retreat House, which they built for people to visit and to listen to amazing stories of conversion, continues to grow. I believe I heard that Patrick has said that it is a never ending project. Nate finally had his first opportunity to hear the testimony of Patrick's conversion from the God of money to the God of Love. Only Patrick can tell that story.

I met a dear young priest, a Father Heiner, at The Castle. He knew a seminarian friend of mine in the US. I apologize to Father if I have not spelled his name correctly. We were halfway around the world when we met and found that we had a friend in common. I feel that soon all of God's children will meet and come together. Right now, many of them are finding each other in Medjugorje.

As we strolled around the beautiful gardens and admired the lovely structures of stone, we met up with Nancy. She graciously invited us to come to lunch with other visitors and with the people who lived and worked there. Nancy is still as warm as she was when I first met her in Seroki Brijeg with Father Jozo. Nate and I have been incredibly blessed with hundreds of friends from all over the world, many of whom we have met in this holy place to which we have been invited by the Mother of God. It is for me the gateway between this earth and our next home in eternity. When I step foot on the soil of Medjugorje, I have a feeling that I am more than halfway there. I hope I get to stay when I arrive at the gates of Heaven.

"Dear Children,

Today I am with you and bless you all with my Motherly Blessing of peace and I urge you to live your life of faith even more, because you are still weak and not humble. I urge you little children to speak less and to work more on your personal conversion so that your witness may be fruitful. And, may your life be an unceasing prayer. Thank you for having responded to my call."

Message: September 25, 2010

20

HOLY GOLD

I COULD NOT END this book without talking about the special gifts that Our Holy Mother gives to all of us in Medjugorje, sometimes before and frequently after we have been there. I have read that you don't even have to even go there to receive one. I just heard recently about people having this gift given to them here at shrines in the United States. You know, I am sure, that I am talking about, the gold rosaries.

At the beginning of this book, I explained that my first rosary, which had been very old with blackened chains, had turned a bright gold as I stood praying at the window the first morning of my first trip. I think I had taken about three rosaries with me. I even told Nate that I was embarrassed that they were all so old and all so tired looking. But, I took them anyway. Usually, when I have something that I like, I keep it and in the case of the rosaries, they had become a part of my life. I didn't buy new ones, I just hung on to those I loved. One was blue glass and it kept coming apart. I had collected about nine of them over the years and I kept them in dresser drawers, in little drawstring bags, in jewelry cases and sometimes in boxes on tables or chests. I came home with one gold rosary that year, as I remember, and in the coming weeks and months,

I kept finding more of them that had turned to a gold color as I came upon them in the places where they were kept. I remember one morning coming upon the blue glass rosary. Not only had the chains turned bright gold, the rosary was fully intact and never fell apart again.

In 2009 we had a fire and our house was destroyed to the point where it had to be completely raised and rebuilt from the ground up. Fire was the major culprit, but water and smoke had also done considerable damage. However, in spite of all the damage, there were things in the house that we were able to recover. My first gold rosary was one of those things. Hanging over the first statue of Our Lady of Medjugorje, which I purchased in 2006, the rosary survived the smoke, water and fire with only a little change in the color of the gold. The statue was damaged by smoke and most of the gold trim on the garments of Our Lady has faded. There were nine gold rosaries on the statues situated at the end of a bar area off our kitchen, eight of which were totally lost along with the statues on which they hung. Eight of the nine were rosaries that I had found in the house, which had changed to gold, even as long as a year after my first trip in 2006.

After all of the rosaries, except one, were gone, I asked Our Holy Mother if she would bless me with another. It did not appear that any of the new ones I had purchased to replace the lost ones would ever change and I had resigned myself to that realization. Two years later, I was going through a plastic box in which much of my costume jewelry had been stored after the fire by the restoration firm. As I went through the bracelets, I came upon a rosary bracelet that had once been silver. I picked it up out of the box and to my surprise it had turned gold. I ran to Nate to show him what I had found. He was as surprised as I was to see that the silver rosary bracelet was now gold. I could not help but wonder just exactly how long ago it had changed.

After the fire, one of my purchases was a lovely silver and crystal rosary from the gift shop of our church. I have to admit that I kept a pretty close eye on it wondering if the chains and the silver caps on each crystal bead would change. I not want to expect this to happen, but it is hard not to look from time to time. One day I looked at it and discovered that it was gold, not a bright gold, but gold. The next day it was silver again and this happened day after day, week after week. Finally one day I asked Our Holy Mother why. I could not help but be curious. Was I not praying enough, was I not praying for the right things, was I doing something wrong? What in the world was causing this phenomenon? I finally decided that perhaps someday I would have an answer and if I didn't, so be it. I accepted that situation as it was.

After boarding the bus that was delivering our group to Medjugorje last year, in 2011, Nate and I sat up front as I always had with Nina. I was asked by Nevis to lead the Chaplet of Divine Mercy. We always pray as we start out on the bus to our destination and Nevis generally leads the prayers, but this time she handed me the microphone. I took my crystal and silver rosary from my purse and began to pray. As I looked down, the rosary slowly changed to gold right before my eyes. The gold got deeper and darker as I watched. I touched Nate's arm. He looked over to where I pointed, smiled and nodded.

I started to cry. I seem to do a lot of that in Medjugorje. Finally, I had to tell everyone on the bus what was happening at that very moment in my hands. All of the old guard on the bus just listened and went on praying. They were used to things like this happening. Father Starbuck, who was new to Medjugorje, must have been shaking his head in wonder as to what was going on up in the front of the bus. I don't know if he had ever heard about the gold rosaries. When he stepped down from the bus in front of Yelka's house I could have sworn that he looked at me and asked, "What are you, a saint or something?" No father, definitely not, I am just one of many millions of pilgrims who come to this miraculous place.

Nate lost his one and only gold rosary in the fire too. Unlike me, he did not have drawers full of rosaries and so when he went off to Medjugorje, he took his only two good rosaries with him. Both were black with silver chains. One of these two was the rosary he received from the Knights of Columbus. There was third one that he put into his suitcase at the last minute. It was very old and parts of it were missing. It had four full decades left and the fifth one consisted of one old bead with broken chains linking it to the rest of the rosary. The pouch he carried it in was very old leather. Nate had no idea where it came from or how long he had it.

When Nate took the first two rosaries along, he was hoping that one would be blessed by Our Holy Mother and that at least one would turn gold. It did not happen. Nate had not seen anything unusual. It appeared that he would not be shown anything miraculous on the trip. That is why I was so happy that he saw the cloud formation of the Virgin and her Child in the sky. It was a beautiful miracle memory that we both could share. Nate told me that throughout the entire trip he was checking to see if either of the good rosaries had undergone a change. They had not. Of course, we know that this is something that we should never expect to happen, but being human continues to be a part of us even in Medjugorje.

We were home a few days and as we gradually got everything unpacked and put away, Nate had a surprise. He took the little leather pouch out of his suitcase and started to put it away. I asked if he had looked at the rosary inside. He had not. He picked it up, opened the case and there it was, the old, worn black rosary with the broken chains and the missing decade, gleaming gold in his hand. He had his gift. However, it was not meant to be with Nate for long. Six months later, it was lost in the fire. We thought it was gone forever, but when I searched through the costume jewelry box, there it was. This time it was in a little plastic bag, black beads almost scorched beyond recognition, its gold chains black again. We kept it. Someday perhaps it will rise from the ashes again and Nate will carry it with him in heaven. We both know there is a heaven and now you do too.

Trying to put into words what one experiences in Medjugorje is difficult even if it is something that you are sharing with one you love in the privacy of your home. Writing about these experiences is almost impossible, because you realize that there will be ridicule and disbelief forthcoming, possibly even from those you love. You may even end up being branded as mentally incompetent and hysterical. And, that is within your own family.

I fully expect to experience a few raised eyebrows when some of the miracle stories are presented to the outside world. If you recall, I was nervous about even sharing my story of seeing heaven as I strolled through the field upon my return from the castle. After all, how many of us see that kind of thing. I certainly know that I have never met anyone who has and if it were not for Jacov, I still would not be sure if I had been hallucinating. I do want readers to know that before I took this leap and began to write, I promised myself and God that I would not exaggerate or bend the truth in any way. I have asked the Holy Spirit to help me keep that promise as he guides my hands on the keys of my computer each day. I want you to know that I do not expect any of you to believe my story. God gave you free will and it is yours as a gift to use as you wish.

Dear Readers,

I have chosen the following message from our Holy Mother to share with those of you who have read this book thus far and have had serious doubts as to my sanity.

Rita Silvestri, Author

"Dear Children,

I look at you and I see in your heart death without hope, with restlessness and anger. There is no prayer or trust in God, that is why The Most High permits me to bring you hope and joy. Open yourselves. Open your hearts to God's mercy and he will give you everything you need and will fill your hearts with peace because he is your peace and your hope. Thank you for having responded to my call."

Message: November 25, 2010

21

THE WALLED CITY

ONE MORE EVENT TOOK place during my first trip to Medjugorje that I hesitated to include in these stories. However, I have had a change of heart and have decided that this is something I should share. As you may recall, I mentioned that we flew into Dubrovnik the first time and that cruise ships travel from all over the world to dock in the port of the city which is known as the Star of the Adriatic. It is for good reason, as I will explain. Toward the end of my visits to Medjugorje, a trip to Dubrovnik was always arranged by our tour leader, Nevis. Pilgrims could decide on their own to visit or not to visit Dubrovnik. At first I hesitated to take the trip feeling that because I had come on the pilgrimage for the sole purpose of spending all of my time in the place where Our Holy Mother had come to bring messages from her son, Jesus. I came to realize however, that Dubrovnik was also a holy place and that there was much to learn there about my faith and the history of the church in this ancient and magnificent walled city built high on the cliffs above the crystal blue waters of the Adriatic.

A bus was chartered and the cost was divided amongst those of us who made the decision to travel the two and a half hour journey. We traversed above the seaside on a road that wound its way through the mountains and beside the shore of one of the most beautiful bodies of water in the world. Since the trip did not include the cost of this extra expedition, we did have to pay not only only for the bus, but for our food and a tip for the driver. The extra cost was worth every single penny each every time I went, the first time on my own and after that with my husband Nate at my side.

Wherever we went somewhere on a bus or in taxis, we prayed as we did while hiking through the fields and vineyards on the way to the village. On my first trip, we were honored to have our dear Laurie explain the history of Dubrovnik. Laurie home schools her children and is a walking encyclopedia of information on all subjects. She knew a great deal about Dubrovnik and made the trip even more interesting with her narrative. We were also blessed to have Father White, our beloved Pilgrim Priest lead us in saying the Rosary and the Chaplet of Divine Mercy both coming and going. In addition, we had the Holy Spirit guiding us along each and every kilometer plus a busload of Guardian Angels keeping us safe as we gazed upon a brilliant sun dancing off the white caps on the sea below. I have seen much of the world and I promise you that there is no other place on earth quite like it.

Because I love the city so much, I would like to go into great detail in describing Dubrovnik, but that would only be with the help of Google and would amount to another book. Let me just give you a few pertinent facts that I have learned to further spark your interest. I strongly suggest that you take the trip to this incredible city if you are able to do so.

Dubrovnik became a city in the sixth century. Archeologists have suggested that there may be an even older city built below the current one, but I have never heard anything about that beyond speculation. Because of its location, being the first protected port that ships would sail into on an east to west route, Dubrovnik became a thriving maritime port and entered a golden age of commerce around the sixteenth century. At that time, the Venetian Empire, the sole enemy of the Dubrovnik Republic began to wane. Dubrovnik then had a proud fleet of 180 to 200 ships of every description. It was also a huge center of culture in the arts and sciences which excelled in literature, poetry, and other fields of culture. It was ruled by its aristocracy. The Republic maintained neutrality for several centuries and had enjoyed a trade route agreement with the Turkish Empire for which it paid a small two percent tariff.

Things, however, were not perfect in the sixteenth century when a devastating earthquake brought Dubrovnik to its knees. Napoleon was responsible for bringing the Dubrovnik Republic to its demise in

1808. In 1991, following the Declaration of Independence by Croatia; Serbian and Montenegrin forces mounted an eight month siege of the City determined to completely destroy the region. Today there still remains evidence of the artillery bombardments that put large gaping holes in the fortress walls surrounding the old city. Photographs of the men and boys who died in the conflict are on display and you become aware that most of the male population from as young as twelve or thirteen was gunned down without mercy. These exhibits depicting the war can be seen in a museum across from the church of St. Blaise.

Today, the glimmering beauty of the white walls rising above the sea in Dubrovnik heralds the new prosperity and return of a bustling tourist industry. Delightful restaurants dot the city and shops with beautiful wares give one the feeling of being back in the golden age of the earlier centuries. It is possible to purchase tickets to walk along the tops of the walls to gaze out toward the white sand beaches across from the old city and wonder at the beauty emanating from every direction. From the top of the walls you can see the homes dating back centuries, many still sought after and occupied. Brilliantly colored laundry dries in the intense sun while children and dogs play in delight. As the saying goes, Dubrovnik is truly candy for the senses.

Much more awaits you in the churches and exhibits hidden here and there and the architecture alone will give you hours a pleasure. St. Blaise is the Patron Saint of Dubrovnik. The church of St. Blaise was originally built in 1667 and destroyed in 1706 by fire. It was rebuilt in the Romanesque design that you see today and holds many treasures of the church. On the roof, next to a magnificent dome, there stands a statue of St. Blaise holding a plan of the city in his arm. St. Blaise is one of my very favorite saints and I have counted on him to keep me safe as long as I can remember. I choke a great deal and look forward each year to his Feast Day, February 3rd when we have our throats blessed by our a priest using the traditional crossed candles for which he is known.

St. Blaise was a physician and a bishop in Turkey. He was martyred by being beaten and then beheaded. He was first referenced in medical writings around the very end of the fifth century. He was known for interceding in cases of throat illness and particularly in curing those who had swallowed fish bones, a common problem in cities near the sea. The church of St. Blaise holds many valuable Christian relics and in front of the right side altar there is a replica of the body of a young Roman soldier who was martyred in the early Christian church. For years I thought this to be the incorrupt body of a Roman saint, but I was told on my last visit that it is thought to be crafted from wax.

During our first visit to the church of St. Blaise, Father White was honored in being able to celebrate mass there. When the mass was over, those of us in attendance were invited to the room behind the altar where we saw beautiful relics and were given the opportunity to purchase the candles used to bless throats in the tradition of St. Blaise. These were not the ones I was familiar with because they were shaped in a U and the bottom sections of the candles were melted and twisted together. Modern day candles are tied together to form a large letter X.

I had an interesting experience at the airport in Vienna on the return flight home. I packed the candles I had purchased as gifts for priest friends in my carry-on bag to keep them from breaking. As I entered security, I was asked to open my bag and then was escorted from the gate to a table. There I was asked to unpack the candles. Apparently the guard was at a complete loss as to what they might be. He might have thought that I planned to light them up and set fire to the seats in the passenger section of the 747. Fortunately, I was not carrying any matches.

In my attempt to describe the use of the candles, I put a set into my left hand and held it up to my neck. That did not ring any bells with the guard who simply stared at me and shook his head. Enter the Holy Spirit, my unceasing guardian and guide. Suddenly I blessed myself in front of my throat with the Sign of the Cross with my right hand. The lights went on in the eyes of the guard who spoke no English. After that, I was directed to put my ridiculous candles back into my bag and move on. One never knows when the Holy Spirit will save us from the gulag. Praise be to God!

In addition to the Church of St. Blaise, there are many other beautiful churches in Dubrovnik, two of which are the Dominican Church and Monastery where the oldest working apothecary in the world can be found. The Cathedral of the Virgin Mary is inside the gates of the old city. The Church of the Holy Annunciation and the Church of the Holy Cross are further down the square. Most are open during the day and I have been to the Cathedral for the noon mass during the week. I understand that there are at least twenty two churches inside the walled city, but I have never found that many or taken the time to count them.

Inside the Cathedral of the Virgin Mary, there is a reliquary which houses ancient relics. We had to purchase tickets to enter this room and only two or three persons are allowed at the same time. Some a date back to the birth of Christ and there is even a piece of cloth which is said to have been taken from a diaper worn by the infant Jesus. Photos are not allowed in the hallowed place and cameras must be checked at the door. To be caught smuggling in a camera is to face immediate expulsion and loss of your camera. The relics are incredibly rare and beautiful and to view them is to step back into ancient times.

One more point. I mentioned shops and restaurants. My husband managed to find every gelato stand on the square. He consumes gigantic cones of many flavors as he peruses the square in the old section of Dubrovnik. He would recommend some flavors, however, he claims that they are all delicious and worth tasting. Additionally, if you would like to visit Dubrovnik, I recommend that you join your fellow pilgrims and head to the airport on the last day of the pilgrimage. Change your reservations and don't get on the plane. The tour company can help with that. Take a taxi back from the airport to the old city to spend another night in Dubrovnik. Nate and I did that one year and spent an extra day just touring on our own. We stayed at a magnificent hotel just up the street from where the busses drop off and pick up pilgrims from their daily tours of the city. I will not provide the name of the hotel because I am not in the travel business, but you know now where it is located, just up the street from the walled city on the right. It is expensive but well worth the cost of a room for one night. Since you are already in Croatia, why not enjoy everything that the country has to offer. Stay a few more days! Oh, and, be sure to try the gelato.

"Dear Children,

God gave you the grace to live and to defend all the good that is in you and around you and to inspire others to be better and holier; but satan too does not sleep and through modernism diverts you and leads you to his ways. Therefore little children, in the love for my Immaculate Heart, love God above everything and live His commandments. In this way, your life will have meaning and peace will rule on earth. Thank you for having responded to my call."

Message: May 25, 2010

22

WHERE THE HEART IS

ACH AND EVERY TIME I have to pack up and ready myself to leave Medjugorje I develop separation anxiety. I have never been able to shake myself of the idea of living next door to Patrick and Nancy and grilling hamburgers with them. The first trip to my heavenly home was no different when it came to leave than any of the others. Same scenario, same anxiety and same thoughts about running through the fields at night and hiding until the bus has pulled away from Yelka's front yard. In fact, it was pretty bad the first time. Getting to Medjugorje can be brutal, but leaving there can be much worse especially since it happens to be a corner of heaven.

I have one last miraculous experience to share. It happened on my last day in Medjugorje the first time I traveled there. Pilgrims go to the Risen Christ with small cotton squares or handkerchiefs. These are used to hold up to and absorb the little drops of oil mixed with water which drip from one of the legs of the bronze figure of Christ on the Cross. For days I had been using tissues and I wanted to do what others were doing so that I could take home some of the drops myself. The tissues were not strong enough. For days I wondered where to buy the squares. As it turned out, they were everywhere.

I finally purchased some and on the last morning of my stay I went to the statue with a cloth in hand only to be told by another pilgrim that the weeping had not occurred for two days. I was heartbroken. I sat down in front of the statue and began to pray. Within minutes I looked up to see little drops of moisture drops forming on the leg and start to drip down one by one in a rosary like fashion. I thanked Jesus for another miracle and held up my little square of cloth to absorb them. I still have the cloth. It was not lost in the fire that destroyed our house in 2009.

It is hard enough to leave any place you love, but then add to it that the planes usually fly out of Dubrovnik, Split or Sarajevo at the crack of dawn. Add one more thing and consider that you have to be at the airport at the very least one hour before the flight leaves. Then, add another hour for safe keeping. Of course, the airport is approximately three hours away. Putting this all together says one thing. Leave early, very early. Knowing that, we all stayed up like a bunch of teenagers on the night of departure because we knew that when we will finally got on the plane we would sleep. That, of course, is very far from true.

Given what my trip to Medjugorje was like the first time, I was more than a little nervous about what the return trip held in store, but that had little or nothing to do with the fact that I didn't want to leave. These were just excuses to stay. I mulled over the obvious thoughts. My husband, my home and my dogs and cats were all in St. George and, of course, my children, grandchildren and all the other members of my family were back in the United States. My clothes and my shoes were there too and, of course, all of my money. It sounded pretty logical to me that when it was time for me to leave, it was time for me to leave. But, when it came to the things that I had witnessed in Medjugorje, the rational approach in my mind was to stay right where I was and invite everybody to come over and join me.

Seriously, I was not thinking that way, but the pull to remain was still there. The pull to be with Our Holy Mother and to lead the life of prayer and goodness had become a part of my daily routine. I loved it.

I loved everything that was Medjugorje and I could not imagine myself leaving it all behind. I have read many accounts from people who have had near death experiences. They see heaven and once that happens, they want to stay. They are sent back to earth essentially kicking and screaming. That is a little bit the way I felt. Why did I have to leave? Why could I not live both lives, here and there?

I lingered in my room at Ivan's as long as I safely could. The front door kept opening and closing as each person also staying there trudged down the stairs with bags in hand and walked the short distance to the bus parked two houses away. Finally, I heard Mary's voice and knew that I had to join her or somebody would send out a search party for me. I picked up my bags and I remember walking quietly down the pitch black street sometime after one in the morning. I put them down a little distance from the bus and waited in the dark with everyone else who was feeling the effects of the early hours of the morning. Nina was there and she got on the bus. After a few minutes I joined her and sat quietly waiting for everyone to arrive. Then, I felt the pull again and got off the bus. I just needed a few more minutes with my feet touching the sacred ground of this place that I loved so much. I was secure in knowing that I would have a place to sit with Nina and that she would never surrender my seat, so I continued to hang back.

I could hear Nevis saying over and over to each person, "be sure you have your passports in your hand as you board". My friend Laurie would not let anyone on the bus without checking each and every hand for the evidence. Apparently, a few years before, a man had left his passport behind and things had become quite difficult for the entire group. I think they had to turn the bus around and go back to the house. Everybody was worried that they would miss their flights. Sounds like me. It is certain that I would never leave mine behind. That's all I think about. This time I had it in my hand. Laurie would be pleased with me. Passports aside, I stood and watched each of my fellow pilgrims get on the bus that night, hugging and kissing everyone. They were all chattering about seeing the entire group the next year and looking forward to bringing back all of their friends and relatives. They were certainly going to bring along more money to spend at Leo's, the jeweler with the best gold prices.

Suddenly, the area got quiet. I was still standing close to my bags as the bus driver took one last long drag on his cigarette. He threw it on the ground then looked at me and said, "Are those your bags?" I answered yes. With that, he took my suitcase with its precious contents of stone rosaries from Charlie's bargain shop, along with the medals, holy cards and the little pebbles that I had gathered from Apparition Hill and tossed it into the cargo hold of the bus. He slammed the door, secured it, and with a look that could fry a fish, told me to get on!

Laurie took her seat. The door closed behind me and I settled into mine. The bus moved into the darkness of the night over the hills toward the Sarajevo airport and the flight home. I didn't break down. I was sure I would. As I sat back in my seat next to Nina and stared out of the window, I murmured under my breath, "I'll be back".

Our Holy Mother speaks to the people of St. James

Parish in Medjugorje

"Dear Children,

You in the parish be converted. This is my other wish That way, all those who come here shall be able to convert. A humble soul shines with purity and beauty because it has come to know the love of God. Only a humble soul becomes heaven because my Son is in it.

Thank you. Again, I implore you to pray for those whom my Son has chosen... These are your shepherds. Thank you for responding to my call"

Message: March 8, 1984

ACKNOWLEDGMENT

I T TOOK ME A long time to decide to write this book about Medjugorje. I was not sure that I possessed the capability to do so. I wanted to share my experiences with others, if only to encourage them to expand their faith in God. As I set about trying to put my stories down on paper, many people in my life spurred me on. If it had not been for them, I might never have mustered up the courage to go down this road.

The first person to get me started was my brother, Ray, a WWII Marine, who one day said to me and I quote: "You write such long emails, why don't you write a book?" He gave me the food for thought that I needed. We all know that when you write a book, you must have something to write about and I felt that I had plenty of material to draw from. I had been to Medjugorje many times and I had met many people. I was sure that I could write an interesting and compelling story. This is how it all started. Wayne Weible authored a book about Medjugorje. Once I read his book, I had to know more and I started looking for people who shared my interest.

Tom Eckroth, a friend from my parish in St. George, UT, went to Medjugorje in the early days of the apparitions during the war in Croatia. When I heard about what Tom and members of his family experienced, I decided that I wanted to go. Tom knew how to get there, who to go with and where to stay. He also had great devotion to Our Lady of Peace in Medjugorje and had organized a Tuesday morning prayer group which I joined.

Before I left, I discovered a beautiful friend in Michelle Winterman. Michelle had been to Medjugorje more than once and had gone alone. She gave me the guidance and courage that I needed to go on my own. When in the coming years my husband, Nate, joined me, Michelle's wisdom was what we needed to get through some of the difficulties we encountered on our journeys. We love you Michelle.

In Medjugorje, the first year, I found many people who added to the tapestry of the stories I shared with you. Father Jim White became many things to me, a confessor, a friend and the person who daily reminded me of why I was there. Mary Rigdon and Nina De La Garza became close and loving friends with whom I experienced so much. Nina kept me from careening off Cross Mountain. Mary taught me about the saving angels who roam Medjugorje.

In the coming years, friends from St. George joined Nate and me on our pilgrimages. Among them were Don and Marianne Rowe. When I wanted to insert photos into the book, Don was there to help. Both Don and Marianne are special friends.

I want everyone who went to Medjugorje with us to know that we are grateful that they joined us and thank them.

Finally, I love and bless my sons, Mark, Chris and Matt. If it had not been for them, I might not have put these words to paper. I thought it would be nice for them to get to know me better through my thoughts and my beliefs. Finally, I want to thank Nate, my husband, for all of his love and support. He has been at my side through this entire time. He was alone for all the months I that I wrote. May God always bless and keep you with me, Nate.

Thank you one and all.

EPILOGUE

I HAVE TRIED TO show you, the reader, that we are not alone here on earth and that Heaven is just on the other side of a very thin veil that separates us from our eternal home. God is so good to us to allow us to have a place like Medjugorje here on earth. I began to feel very close to God when I lived in South East Asia back in the late 1990s. For the first time I really looked at people of other races who spoke differently than I. They worshipped differently than I, but their love was the same.

I would walk each evening with my husband along a seawall just below the building where we lived and I would watch the parents as they played with their children. The pride in their eyes and the expressions of concern for their little ones were the same as those of mine when my sons were little. I could see that they carefully kept their babies from harm. They taught them to walk. They worried when their children ran ahead and started to disappear into the crowd, just as I did as a young mother.

God, Our Father, is like that. We, as earthly parents, learned from Him. He watches over us. He wants us to be good, to follow His Commandments and to live kind and loving lives. He wants us to be happy. We want our children to be happy and we think that we know exactly what is good for them. We teach what we can teach, then, we step aside and allow them to live as they choose, just as God does with us.

God gave us free will. He cuts us loose and the rest is up to us. He also went an extra mile. He sent his only Son, Jesus Christ to walk among us to show us the Way, His Way. God's only Son died for our salvation. God has also done something else. He has given us His Holy Spirit to guide us on earth, to walk beside us and to show us how to live. He has given us his written Word in the Bible. Above all, he has sent us Mary, Our Mother, the Bride of the Holy Spirit, the Virgin Mother of Jesus. She walks among us here on earth to bring us His messages.

She has been coming here for centuries. There are many famous places in this world where shrines have been erected in memory of the holy events that took place there. Have you heard of Lourdes in France or

Fatima in Portugal? The Shrine of Garabandal is in Spain, and millions of Pilgrims have traveled to the Mexican Shrine of Guadalupe in Mexico City. I have named only a few locations on earth where Mary has come to be with her children to spread the word of her Son. The Catholic Church now has an approved apparition site right here in the United States in Wisconsin, in the small town Champion near Green Bay. Everybody knows where Green Bay is, but did you know that Mary, the Mother of God does too? Apparitions and miracles began there in the late 1800s. Just recently the site was approved by the local bishop. We now have our very own apparition church approved shrine right on our own soil and we can all go there to be with her. It does not require anyone in the US to fly over an ocean and it is not as costly or difficult to go there. If you cannot visit Medjugorje, how about going to Green Bay?

With the world in dire straits such as it is today, Mary has come to all of us to teach us how to gain eternity with God. After all, Christ allowed Himself to be tortured, scourged and nailed to the cross, all to gain eternal life for us. His Mother, our mother, is here to remind us of His sacrifice for mankind. She intercedes with God so that we can all enter heaven when we die. I shared with you that I personally witnessed a glimpse of heaven. I want you to know that I certainly want to go there and I am working daily to prepare for the end of my life here on earth when I will come face to face with Jesus. He is our final judge. He is also Our Savior and Redeemer. We ignore Him on earth. We skip church for sports and the beach. Someday, you and I will present to Him our lives, all of which were filled with failings and sins and we will ask His forgiveness. He just might ask you who you are. You may want to spend some time with Him in His house and get to know Him better.

His mother says in Medjugorje and I quote: "I come to convert you for the last time". Our Lady has been coming throughout the ages. She has always continued to return. Now she is saying that this is the last time, so it sounds to me as though we do not have a lot of time left. Will you be ready if He calls tomorrow? Think about it and bow your head in prayer.

"Dear Children,

In a special way this evening I am calling you to perseverance in trials. Consider how the Almighty is still suffering today on account of your sins. So, when sufferings come, offer them up as a sacrifice to God. Thank you for having responded to my call."

Message: March 29, 1984

FROM THE AUTHOR

Those who travel to Medjugorje, are given a very special gift by Our Holy Mother.

The gift is to be allowed to bestow her motherly blessing upon you. I offer this gift to everyone who has read this book.

May the blessing of Our Holy Mother be upon you and may the Holy Spirit always be with you. Amen

www.ingramcontent.com/pod-product-compliance
Lightning Source LLC
Chambersburg PA
CBHW051315120626
46547CB00015B/2239